CROSS**CURRENTS**
PURSUING SOCIAL JUSTICE AND INTERRELIGIOUS WORK
SINCE 1950

CrossCurrents (ISSN 0011-1953; online ISSN 1939-3881) connects the wisdom of the heart with the life of the mind and the experiences of the body. The journal is operated through its parent organization, the Association for Public Religion and Intellectual Life (APRIL), an interreligious network of academics, activists, artists, and community leaders seeking to engage the many ways religion meets the public. Contributions to the journal exist at the nexus of religion, education, the arts, and social justice. The journal is published quarterly on behalf of the Association for Public Religion and Intellectual Life by the University of North Carolina Press.

The Association for Public Religion and Intellectual Life (formerly ARIL) is a global network of leaders, scholars, and social change agents who explore religious life, engage in intellectual inquiry, and lead ethical action in the world today. Their primary objective, especially through annual summer colloquia and *CrossCurrents*, is to bring together leading voices of our time to advocate for justice and to examine global spiritual and interreligious currents in both historical and contemporary perspectives.

A membership to APRIL includes access to *CrossCurrents* starting with Volume 58, 2008, though our partners at Project MUSE, monthly newsletters, early access to summer colloquium themes, a 40% on UNC Press books, and more. For more information, including membership and subscription rates, visit www.aprilonline.org.

This reissue of *CrossCurrents* was one of four issues published in 2009 as part of Volume 59. For a current masthead visit www.aprilonline.org.

© 2009 Association for Public Religion and Intellectual Life. All rights reserved.

ISBN 978-1-4696-6679-2 (Print)

CROSS CURRENTS

EDITORIAL

4
Global Prophet and Ecumenical Contemplative
Glenn Crider and Victor A. Kramer

ORIGINAL ARTICLES

6
Authentic Identity Is Prayerful Existence
Glenn Crider

7
Prayer and Identity (Transcript of a taped conference)
Thomas Merton

15
Centering Prayer and Attention of the Heart
Cynthia Bourgeault

28
Thomas Merton's Inclusivity and Ecumenism: Silencing the Gong and Cymbals
John Wu, Jr.

49
Going East with Merton: Forty Years Later—And Coming West with Paramahansa Yogananda Today
Emile J. Farge

69
"Fine and Dangerous": Teaching Merton
David A. King

88
A Bibliographical Note: Merton's Complete Journal as Emblem of the Spiritual Journey
Victor A. Kramer and Glenn Crider

BOOKS

90
Signs of Peace: The Interfaith Letters of Thomas Merton
William Apel

92
Cold War Letters
Thomas Merton

94
Notes on Contributors

On the Cover: Drawing by Thomas Merton. Used with permission of the Merton Legacy Trust and the Thomas Merton Center at Bellarmine University.

EDITORIAL

GLOBAL PROPHET AND ECUMENICAL CONTEMPLATIVE

This second gathering of Thomas Merton–related material is by authors we have come to know through our scholarly work publishing *The Merton Annual: Studies in Culture, Spirituality and Social Concerns*. That annual publication about Merton-related studies is now sponsored by The International Thomas Merton Society.

Cynthia Bourgeault's essay, as well as the transcription of Thomas Merton's pointed remarks about prayer and authentic existence, both appeared in our Volume 20. The other essays by Emile Farge, John Wu, and David King are newly conceived articles done expressly for this *CrossCurrents* project, while these three authors have all contributed to *The Merton Annual* in the past. The bibliographical note about Merton's journals suggests the value of that vast project. Our review-essay by Paul Dekar is built from two pieces in *The Merton Annual*.

Readers of *CrossCurrents* may wish to look at back volumes of *The Merton Annual* (Vols. 1–5, AMS Press; Vols. 6–10, Liturgical Press; Vols. 11–16, Sheffield/Continuum; and Vols. 17 and ff, Fons Vitae of Kentucky Press) because it is a refereed publication of scholarship about Merton and Merton-related inquiries which in many ways parallels the continuing work of Joseph Cunneen; the Association for Religion and the Intellectual Life as well as the work now being done by *CrossCurrents* which is cross-cultural and seeded by inter-faith dialogue. Such is also the case with the work of The International Thomas Merton Society which hosts a "General Meeting" every two years. Its Eleventh General Meeting will be held at Nazareth College this year on June 11th through the 14th. The forthcoming Volume 21 of *The Merton Annual* (2009) contains revised and expanded materials from the Tenth (2007) Meeting in Memphis.

Volume 22, under the editorship of David Belcastro and Gray Matthews will include essays about Merton and Poetry (2010).

We are grateful to be editors for both of these issues of *CrossCurrents*. Called Merton "Global Prophet" for the first issue, and here "Ecumenical Contemplative," these titles signal our enthusiasm for Merton's current importance. We think Merton's contributions to spirituality, to the work of love, to the development of wider understanding between, and among world religions, is being furthered by this work.

–Glenn Crider and Victor A. Kramer

AUTHENTIC IDENTITY IS PRAYERFUL EXISTENCE
A Short Commentary

This tape, carefully transcribed and edited by Brother Daniel Carrere, O.C.S.O., was recorded by Thomas Merton during the last years of his life while he was living as a hermit. In its simplicity, it does many valuable things. Above all, Merton reminds his listener that prayer cannot be a project which we undertake. Prayer is, in fact, always initiated by the mystery of God's presence. Prayer is a call just as any vocation is a call. Such a call is not initiated by us as individuals. Rather, it is something an individual hears and to which that person responds. Merton reminds us that no baby is ever aware of its nature and therefore no newborn consciously seeks to act as a baby should act. The child simply *is*—and in being so, the actions of the child are not different than our own entering into all life and prayer. Merton's analogy is to breathing. We do not consciously seek to breathe. We just do this natural action. So, he insists, should our prayer-life be—something which comes as a most natural part of our life. There are things which can be done to inspire the conditions of breathing and there are different kinds of moments when our breathing is different; yet Merton implies the best we can do is to realize there is no one single formula for prayer. Circumstances allow each person to pray in different ways—sometimes liturgically, sometimes in awe and silence. "Successful" prayer is not something to be evaluated.

Glenn Crider

COMMENTARY

Prayer and Identity[1] (Transcript of a taped conference)

A few things on the life of prayer...Do we know why we want to live lives of prayer? Are we praying in such a way that our prayer is simply for "something else"? It's all very well to pray for intentions, and to pray for the world, and to pray for health and all those things; still, a life of prayer tends to be an end in itself. It is right for prayer to be an end in itself insofar as it is entirely centered on God, who is our end, if we can still use those terms—I suppose people still believe that God is our end, in the sense of the goal toward which we orient all our lives, or should orient all our lives.

As religious we still think of our religious life as a life given to God, consecrated to God, oriented to God; and it is in prayer that we are most dedicated, consecrated, and oriented to God. In prayer everything in us is, so to speak, centered on God. It is in prayer that we are most ourselves, that we are most what we want to be, what we hope to be, what we are called to be. But this can easily become very confused, especially if we have some sort of implicit, confused ideas about what our prayer is all about, or what God is all about, and what kind of a thing the religious life is all about. When we are mixed up on these points everything tends to get mixed up, and prayer can become a very mixed-up and frustrating thing when it should be quite simple.

Basically, prayer should be as simple as breathing, as simple as living, but when we make a great issue out of prayer it tends to become confusing; it tends to get distorted. It becomes a cause, the great "cause of prayer," and then it becomes opposed to something else which is not prayer. You get into this break: prayer is something sacred and other things are secular, and you have to keep them apart—and that's a confusion.

As breathing is neither sacred nor secular—you just breathe—so prayer too should be neither sacred nor secular. I do not regard prayer as a specifically sacred activity. It's *life*; it is our life; it comes from the very ground of our life. I think it becomes a sacred activity when it gets to be quite public and formal and so forth, but we should not divide prayer against the rest of our life, and we should not make prayer a cause for which we are willing to fight and have crusades, so to speak. The danger is that our religious life, our prayer, our apostolate—things like that—become causes which we make to serve ourselves. We use them, perhaps, out of a spirit of self-glorification.

Anyway, let's start with the basic proposition that we belong to God, and we want to belong to God, and we want to affirm our belonging to God. We want to live in a consciousness that we belong to him. The great thing in our life is this awareness of our identity as children of God: he is our Father and we live in this constant relationship with him, with him from whom we come, to whom we return, to whom we belong. We belong to him most completely in prayer, and prayer should be the activity, therefore, in which we are most ourselves.

Right away we see that when prayer is not what it should be it becomes the activity when we are most *not* ourselves, when we are *least* ourselves. If we're not praying as we should, we are most artificial in prayer, and we feel that when we are praying we are phony in a certain sense; we're pretending. Of course, this is something we should at times feel because as soon as prayer becomes too much of a project, we do tend to pretend. Rather than praying, we pretend that we're praying. We discover some kind of a role, some part to play; we find some particular kind of prayer that we think we ought to furnish to God and we put ourselves in that role and try to act the part of somebody praying in that particular way. Well, then it's artificial, and one of the great curses of the life of prayer is that when it becomes a role (one learns how to play the part of a religious praying—I am so-and-so and I am praying—or worse still, the role of having a certain degree of prayer, which is all nonsense, and I put myself in that role and I play that) it gets to be very artificial.

This brings up the question of the understanding of ourselves, which is a big question today. Rightly or wrongly, whether we like it or not, we tend to be constantly questioning our understanding of ourselves and who we are, our vocation and whether we should stay or leave, whether we should consider ourselves this way or that way, whether we should look at ourselves from this or that point of view. We have a great variety of choices of identity offered to us today, and we tend to waver around which one are we going to be. We've got all these roles and we don't know which one we're supposed to be in. Well, if you don't know what role you're supposed to be in, you're having a hard time.

It isn't a question of a role; it's a question of a vocation. A vocation is not a role; it's not a part we play. It is a response to a personal call. God speaks and we answer. He doesn't give us a role; the function of being a child of God is not a part that we play; it's not a role. When a baby is born he doesn't start playing the role of baby. He doesn't know he's got a role to play—he hasn't.

This is a big problem. We are obsessed with this idea of understanding ourselves, and it's unavoidable that we are so, but we get that mixed up with prayer. We start trying to understand ourselves in prayer. Prayer becomes a time devoted to self-understanding, evaluation of ourselves; how are we doing? Well, that's what it should not be. It gets to be that to some extent, but we have to try to avoid this because it's wasteful, frustrating, and it's not what we want to do; it's not what prayer's for.

On the contrary, prayer should help us abandon ourselves, to be *not* occupied with ourselves, and to attain to a kind of wholeness, a kind of all-round acceptance, which I would say is a very important fruit of prayer—an all-round acceptance: acceptance of ourselves, acceptance of the world as it is, acceptance of our religious life as it is, not as it *may* some day be or we hope it will be (we have to accept it as it is if we are going to make it what it is going to be); and we really have to accept other people. Prayer is the great way of getting ourselves opened up to this attitude of acceptance and availability and not lamenting our lot so much—just being in it, being with it, being all there, and being ourselves. At the same time, we do have to recognize the fallenness and ambiguity of our state, the fallenness and ambiguity of our love.

The natural material of our prayer is our love, our capacity to love, our human heart. It's most important that our human heart as a whole should function in prayer. In some of the ancient monastic traditions the first thing about prayer is the ability to find one's heart, to seek and find one's own heart, one's true voice to speak to God with and to listen to God with, a true *center*—and not to be ambiguous about this. The fallen state that we are in is that we're ambiguous about our own heart.

To be in a fallen state is to be in a state where one's heart is double, self-contradictory. Even though we're baptized, and even though we are nourished with the bread of life, we maintain this state of ambiguity in spite of ourselves, at least psychologically. We can't get out of it altogether; we have to be saints before we are through with that, and even the saints aren't through with it. We also have to accept this fallenness and ambiguity of our love and of our hearts.

We come to prayer with ambiguous hearts, and we have in ourselves the same doubts as other people to some extent. We are not safely walled off from the world in a little religious universe where everything is secure. Our faith is not secure in the modern world, not that the modern world attacks our faith but that we are simply modern people and therefore ambiguous, and therefore, we tend to doubt. We don't have the simple, direct faith that people of another, less complicated, age were able to have, and we don't have to have that simple, direct faith. We are bound to have a certain element of doubt in our lives because we are ambiguous people, and it is simplicity to recognize this and not to pretend that we are totally out of it. Of course some are more simple and less complicated than others. You don't have a duty to be ambiguous. I'm not saying that your whole life has to become that of playing the role of an ambiguous, doubting person; but with the sincerity that we have in our own hearts, we must respond to God in prayer.

It is God who calls us to prayer. So prayer, first of all, is a response to a call from God, a personal call from God, and I think we should look at it that way even though we don't feel like praying. Let's admit that very often we don't feel like praying and that there are a lot of other things we'd rather do than pray.

God calls us to prayer, and he calls us to the particular kind of prayer that he wants of us. Some he calls to say the psalms; others he calls to a kind of loving attention to him; others he calls to biblical meditation on his word, deepening one's understanding of his word, one's identification with his love and loving will in his word. To learn how to pray is to learn how to respond to God's personal call to us to prayer, and of course the great place for learning this is in the public prayer of the Church, in the liturgy, and in the Bible.

Prayer is an inner awakening, the awakening of an inner self that God intends us to be and to have. It's an awakening of a God-intended self. Guardini has some good things on this in his book on Pascal.[2]

He talks about yielding to the call of God to prayer and the change that happens when one yields to this call and one answers God's call to come to prayer, which is a personal call that we have to listen for. Perhaps the beginning of all prayer (you aren't hit by a thunderbolt and immediately start praying) should be a certain amount of listening and praying that we may hear. When we begin the public prayer of the Church we say, "Lord, open Thou my lips"; well, let's perhaps think of our own meditative prayers as, "Lord, open my ears; open the ears of my heart so that I may hear you calling me to pray"—but the mere fact that I begin to pray is a call to prayer.

Guardini says that if the heart yields to the call, then something happens to it: for the first time appears the genuine center. The *genuine* center, the counterpart of the divine center that is calling, for the first time awakens—the genuine God-intended self, the real self. So what we are aiming for in prayer—right now I'm talking especially of meditative prayer—is this awakening of a genuine center, an authentic personal center that is the counterpart to the divine center that is calling. They are both within us, and yet we don't find them by introspection. Introspection is usually not helpful for prayer.

In this opening up and acceptance of God's call in our genuine center, our depth, Guardini says, the mystery of that absolute initiative by which God reveals himself gives light, touches the bottom of the heart so effectively that it unbinds itself, opens, and recovers sight and freedom. So, a further development in our life of prayer is this interior opening up, this unbinding of the inner self at the touch of God, to recover sight and above all to recover freedom.

The *great* thing that we are all seeking today, especially in the Church, is this freedom of the sons of God, and there is no freedom of the sons of God without prayer. So when this unbinding of the inner self takes place and we are, so to speak, liberated—liberated for what?—liberated to go to God, liberated to have free access to God and free speech with God (*parrhesia*, confident free speech), to have access to God and speak to him face to face in the dark (so to speak), to speak to him as sons to a father with all confidence and without any fear. Without *any* fear, except of course that reverential fear that gives us a deep *respect* for God as infinite, incomprehensible Presence—and yet without fear.

God wishes us to speak to him without fear, even though we are sinners, with perfect loving confidence as his children. This is what he asks us to come to prayer for: that we may walk right up to him without fear and say, "You are my father; I love you," and whatever else we believe that he wishes us to say. It isn't just that he dictates to us things to say; what we say to him comes from our own heart. We can invent new things to say to him, if there are things to say, and we can say nothing; we can just listen. There are many things we can do in the creative and inventive situation that is our mutual understanding with God in prayer. He wishes to establish us in a relationship of mutual understanding, realizing that he understands us and we understand him. He understands us to some extent in a way that we can understand: we know that he has a father's understanding of us and we know what that is. It's not purely a mysterious, totally incomprehensible dark night of the soul thing, except sometime it is.

All these things we can confidently keep in mind as realities of the world of prayer.

This opening to God is an opening also to everything else. The Presence of God, which is so mysterious and so real and so intimate, does not exclude anything else; it doesn't block out other things necessarily, although sometimes it seems to. It also opens us to embrace the whole of life, the whole of the world. It opens us to everyone and to everything, and we embrace everyone and everything in God.

Of course here we come to the problem of the new consciousness of modern man, which is such a great problem because it is our problem to a great extent.[3] We all have this problem of modern man for whom, as they say, God is dead. Of course that can mean all kinds of things. It may mean just that modern man is unable to conceive God in any way and remains inarticulate before him. [Then there is] the so-called self-withholding of God that somebody has spoken of: that modern man is inevitably in a position where God withholds himself from modern man. But is this true? This is no dogma of faith; this is no axiom. We know that God does not withhold himself; but people who are too influenced by what other people are saying are soon going to be running around saying God is simply inaccessible to any of us: what's the use of trying to pray, what's the use of anything like this; we must find God in some totally different way—because he withholds himself we have no access to him, and so forth. This is not true; it just simply is not true, and we as Christians realize that even though we may at times have moments of great dryness and desolation and so forth and so forth, it doesn't mean a thing. God does not withhold himself from his children. We have received his Spirit; we live in Christ. Does God withhold himself? He gives us the Body and Blood of his Son. What do you mean, withholds himself? We don't need feelings of consolation to realize that God gives himself.

To confuse God's giving of himself with feelings of consolation, that's—well, it's an old-time mistake; we know that's delusive. But we have to realize that God is an infinitely higher reality than we are, and when a higher reality meets a lower one, Guardini says, this occurs in such a way that the higher reality appears questionable from the point of view of the lower reality, so we instinctively doubt God. It's understood that we *are* creatures of doubt, but doubt and faith in a certain way can coexist in the same person—not real theological doubt but *questioning*, self-questioning above all. We must not confuse our self-questioning with our questioning of God, our self-doubt with our doubt of God. We come to God in prayer with a great deal of doubt of ourselves, a great deal of doubt of our own authenticity, and we should because we're not totally authentic, but that should not become also a doubt of God.

Nevertheless, when we do come face to face with him we find that he is questionable from our point of view, until faith breaks through and, by his gift, that question is resolved: not by our figuring, not by our reasoning, not by our reading, and not by somebody else telling us, but simply by God resolving the difficulty.

On the other hand, if one consistently holds to a lower reality against a higher, one may develop a state of radical bad faith in which, constantly being suspicious of the higher reality, constantly questioning it and constantly rejecting it and pushing it away, there is formed a bad conscience. The doubt is suppressed and you get a doubt in another form now, the doubt that after all it may be something totally beyond us that is there and is speaking to us, and so forth, and we refuse to hear. This produces a state of resentment and a kind of inner bitterness and bad faith that we try to overcome with a sort of false liberty and resentment.

Sometimes this happens to a modern person, a person dominated by the way other people think, and by the way society thinks, and by the general agnosticism of the world in which we live, which is a normal thing today. You just can't avoid it; it's there. Dominated too much by this, we can't allow ourselves to really let go and believe, and yet we know somehow in us, in the depths of our being, something is calling us to believe; yet we can't do it. And so we hold back and then we're guilty about it and we accuse ourselves and then perhaps we are guilty and perhaps we don't believe.

The great thing is to get away from this preoccupation with ourselves, examining ourselves, examining our prayer, examining our good faith and our bad faith and our faith, and whether we believe and whether we don't believe, and whether God loves us and whether he doesn't love us—and all that stuff—and simply abandon our preoccupation with ourselves and let go, because "He that would save his life must lose it, and he that would lose his life for my sake will save it,"[4] and that is the important thing.

– *Thomas Merton*

Notes

1. Transcribed and edited by Ernest Daniel Carrere, O.C.S.O. The original and longer taped conference, generically titled "On Prayer" (no date), is available at the Thomas Merton Center of Bellarmine University in Louisville, Kentucky. The tape was prepared by Merton for cloistered nuns in Louisville.
2. Guardini, Romano, *Pascal for Our Time*, trans. Brian Thompson (New York: Herder and Herder), 1966.
3. See Merton, Thomas, *Faith and Violence* (Notre Dame, IN: University of Notre Dame Press, 1968), Part 4.
4. Mt 16:25; Lk 9:24

CENTERING PRAYER AND ATTENTION OF THE HEART

Cynthia Bourgeault

In the thirty years now since Centering Prayer first moved beyond the walls of St. Joseph's Abbey in Massachusetts and became a lay groundswell, it has certainly implanted itself deeply and (one hopes) permanently in the canon of Christian contemplative practice. Yet it still jostles somewhat uneasily against the walls of received tradition. I am not speaking here of fundamentalist-generated fear ("The devil will get you if you make your mind a blank"), but rather, of serious reservations on the part of some deeply formed in the Christian contemplative tradition that this prayer is somehow "breaking the rules." In its classic presentations, Christian prayer is "progressive"; it passes through stages. And the contemplative stage is traditionally regarded as the highest, or most subtle. In the concluding words of a recent, thoughtful article by a well-prepared commentator, "One does not take the kingdom by force."[1] Contemplation is approached by a gradual path leading from purgative to illuminative to unitive; from cataphatic to apophatic. The "ladder" of spiritual ascent is so deeply engrained on the Christian religious imagination that it seems virtually impossible to conceive of the journey in any other way. Contemplative prayer is "higher," and it is approached only gradually through a long journey of purification and inner preparation.

But is this in fact really so?

"You have to experience duality for a long time until you see it's not there," said Thomas Merton at a conference given to the nuns of the Redwoods shortly before boarding the plane to Asia on the last leg of his human journey. "Don't consider dualistic prayer on a lower level. The lower is higher. There are no levels. At any moment you can break through to the underlying unity which is God's gift in Christ. In the end, Praise praises. Thanksgiving gives thanks. Jesus prays. Openness is all."[2]

Certainly, these words of unitive, realized mastery make it clear that Merton "got there." But how? Was this breakthrough insight the result of his long tread up the traditional ladder of ascent—in other words, is he "exhibit A" of the assertion that the classic monastic model works? Or is his unitive awakening something more akin to Dorothy in the final scene of *The Wizard of Oz*, when she realizes that all along the shoes that would carry her home have been right there on her feet?

This is, of course, an impossible question to answer, and I do not intend to do so directly; only to use it as a kind of leverage. In the words of the poet Philip Booth, "How you get there is where you arrive," and Merton's journey could only have been Merton's. And yet the door, once he found it, can only be seen as the timeless and universal gate. Like a few others before him and a few significant monastic others following in his wake (Thomas Keating most prominently), he simply, in my estimate, came upon that hidden back door or "wormhole" within the Christian path that transports one out of the "progressive" journey in linear time into the instantaneous, seamless fullness from which prayer is always emerging.

And he found it in the same way that all who find it do so: in the gathering awareness that the cave of the heart is entered not only or even primarily through purification and concentration, but through surrender and release. This is this hidden, backdoor path that I wish to explore in the following essay. My thesis is that there has always been an alternative within Christian spiritual practice to the "ladder of ascent": perhaps not as well known, but fully orthodox and in the end even more reliable, since it derives, ultimately, from the direct teaching and self-understanding of Jesus himself. It is from this alternative pathway that Centering Prayer derives its legitimacy and its powerful capacity to heal and unify.

Centering prayer as self-emptying love

First, let me give a quick summary of Centering Prayer, for those unfamiliar with its somewhat unusual methodology. As a method of meditation situated within the Christian contemplative tradition, Centering

Prayer is founded entirely on the gesture of surrender, or letting go. The theological basis for this prayer lies in the principle of *kenosis* (Philippians 2:6–11), Jesus's self-emptying love that forms the core of his own self-understanding and life practice. During the prayer time itself, surrender is practiced through the letting go of thoughts as they arise. Unlike other forms of meditation, neither a focused awareness nor a steady witnessing presence is required. There is no need to "follow" the thoughts as they arise; merely to promptly let them go as soon as one realizes he or she is engaged in thinking (a "Sacred Word" is typically used to facilitate this prompt release).

With committed practice, this well-rehearsed gesture of release is inwardly imprinted and begins to coalesce as a distinct "magnetic center" within a person; it can actually be experienced on a subtle physical level as a "drop and release" in the solar plexus region of the body and as a tug to center. Of its own accord it begins to hold a person at that place of deeper spiritual attentiveness during prayer time. Not long after this initial "tethering of the heart" has set in, most experienced practitioners begin to feel the tug even outside their times of prayer, in the midst of their daily rounds, reminding them of the deepening river of prayer that has begun to flow in them beneath the surface of their ordinary lives. The intent of Centering Prayer is not to "access" God through contemplative stillness or mystical experience, but to teach its practitioners how to align spontaneously with Jesus's own continuously creative and enfolding presence through emulating his kenotic practice in all life situations.

Thus, the real measure of this prayer is not found during the prayer time itself; Centering Prayer neither seeks nor accepts[3] what is commonly known as "mystical experience." Instead, it is found in the gradual but steady capacity to conform a person to "the mind of Christ," and the life attitudes of compassion, generosity, and freedom that flow from this gesture.

"God should be with you like a toothache!" proclaimed the nineteenth-century mystic Theophan the Recluse.[4] And while most of us might have preferred a different metaphor, it does speak forcefully to the fact that our concept of God is *sensate*. Remembrance of God is not a mental concept; it exists deeply embodied as a vibration, a homing frequency to which we can become increasingly sensitively attuned.

This growing experiential awareness of magnetic center is very important, not only for one's spiritual development but because of the new light it sheds on the ancient and venerable *desideratum* of the Western spiritual path: the goal of "putting the mind in the heart." As I hope to show, it is against this backdrop that Centering Prayer's powerful and innovative contribution to the received wisdom of Western spirituality becomes fully visible. But let us return to Merton.

The way of the heart
It is by now established that during the final decade of his life Merton was deeply drawn not only to Buddhism, but equally to Sufism, that mystical arm of Islam in which so much of the original heart and flavor of Jesus's Near-Eastern kenotic spirituality came to reside.[5] In particular, during those years, he had come upon Louis Massignon's commentary on a treatise on the heart by al-Hallâj, a ninth century Sufi saint. Merton refers to this writing both in his journals and throughout his *Conjectures of a Guilty Bystander* (1966), and Massignon's vision of the "point vierge," that mysterious liminal ground equally shared between creator and created, forms the basis for those stirring final paragraphs of "A Member of the Human Race":

> Then it was as if I suddenly saw the secret beauty of their hearts, the depths of their hearts where neither sin nor desire nor self-knowledge can reach, the core of their reality...Again that expression, *le point vierge* (I cannot translate it) comes in here. At the center of our being is a point of nothingness which is untouched by sin and by illusion, a point of pure truth, a point or spark which belongs entirely to God, which is never at our disposal, from which God disposes of our lives, which is inaccessible to the fantasies of our own mind or the brutalities of our own will. This little point of nothingness and of *absolute poverty* is the pure glory of God in us. It is so to speak His name written in us, as our poverty, as our indigence, as our dependence, as our sonship. It is like a pure diamond, blazing with the invisible light of heaven. It is in everybody, and if we could see it we would see these billions of points of light coming together in the face and blaze of a sun that would make all the darkness and cruelty of life vanish completely.[6]

CYNTHIA BOURGEAULT

Merton's intuitive mystical grasp of this teaching contexts it faultlessly, it seems, within the lineage of the Christian *via negativa*. But so seamless and evocative is his transposition that one may overlook the fact that the passage also has a context within its own Islamic frame of reference. This "point of nothingness and of absolute poverty" within al-Hallâj's treatise is in fact the *sirr,* the final veil covering the heart.[7] What looks like a mystical metaphor within Merton's prose-poetry actually belongs to a rigorous anatomy of the heart as a spiritual instrument of perception—or, as Massignon puts it, "the Quranic notion that the heart is the organ prepared by God for contemplation."[8] And it is just here that the point becomes interesting. For as one conceives the heart, so one conceives the transformative journey.

With regard to this "Quaranic notion of the heart," perhaps the clearest elucidation comes from a modern Sufi master, Kabir Helminski. In his *Living Presence* Helminski writes:

> We have subtle subconscious faculties we are not using. Beyond the limited analytic intellect is a vast realm of mind that includes psychic and extrasensory abilities, intuition; wisdom; a sense of unity; aesthetic, qualitative, and symbolic capacities. Though these faculties are many, we give them a single name with some justification because they are operating best when they are in concert. They comprise a mind, moreover, in spontaneous connection with the cosmic mind. This total mind we call "heart."[9]

The heart's job is to look deeper than the surface of things, deeper than the jumbled, reactive landscape of our ordinary awareness, and to beam in on the deeper, ensheltering spiritual world in which our being is truly rooted (Jesus calls it "the Kingdom of Heaven"). As the heart becomes clearer and stronger, we are able to come into alignment with divine being and are able to live authentically the dance of divine self-disclosure which is our true self. Helminski goes on to explain:

> The heart is that antenna that receives the emanations of subtler levels of existence. The human heart has its proper field of functioning beyond the reactive, superficial ego-self. Awakening the heart, or the Spiritualized mind, is an unlimited process of making

the mind more sensitive, focused, energized, subtle and refined, of joining it to its cosmic milieu, the infinity of love.[10]

It is clear that Merton absorbed this basic concept of the heart as an organ of spiritual perception—the whole "antenna" aspect—and was deeply impressed with it. In his marvelous lectures on Sufism to the novices of Gethsemani, he speaks over and over of that "little kernel of gold" (Massignon's *le point vierge*, al-Hallaj's *sirr*), which is not only our deepest reality, but also a kind of homing signal through which we can stay aligned with that reality. As he sees it,

> The real freedom is to be able to come and go from that center, and to be able to do without anything that is not connected to that center. Because when you die, that is all that is left. When we die, everything is destroyed except this one thing, which is our reality that God preserves forever. He will not permit its final destruction.
>
> And the thing is, that we know this. This is built into that particular little grain of gold, this spark of the soul, or whatever it is. It *knows* this. And the freedom that matters is the capacity to be in contact with that center. For it is from that center that everything else comes.[11]

But make no mistake: Merton is not embracing an Islamic anthropology; rather, in the mirror of Sufism he is able to recognize the heart he has already come to know intimately through his years of Christian contemplative practice. And in that same moment of recognition, he also understands intuitively that the way to remain in contact with "that little grain of gold, this spark of the soul" is simply to be able to let go of whatever it is that jams its signal.

Surmounting love by love
For most Western Christians, the heart would more readily be associated with the capacity to *feel*. Its genius is emotional empathy. Even that old pop psychology cliché, "being in the heart" versus "being in the head," rests on our staunch conviction that the heart mirrors the real person

through its capacity to feel, to love, to empathize. If it has a capacity for spiritual perception, it is exercised through love. Hence the immortal instructions in the *Cloud of Unknowing*: "God may be reached and held fast by means of love, but by means of thought never."[12]

It is not surprising, then, that overwhelmingly in the Western tradition, the core methodology for "putting the mind in the heart" can be described as *the concentration of affectivity*. In both the Christian East and the Christian West, the basic strategy for spiritual transformation begins by engaging the heart's natural capacity to feel. Once the heart has been stirred by strong emotions, it is a surprisingly short step to concentrate and purify these emotions through spiritual practice and harness their vibrant energy for spiritual awakening.

You can see the strategy already at work in John Cassian in the fifth century, particularly in his Tenth Conference, where he urges the continuous use of the prayer sentence from Psalm 70, "O Lord, come to my assistance, Oh God make speed to save me." Cassian goes on to explain: "It is not without good reason that this verse has been chosen from the whole of Scripture as a device. It carries within it all the feelings of which human nature is capable."[13] By embracing the full intensity of these feelings, an ardor is generated that catapults the heart free and clear of its egocentric orbit and straight into the heart of God.

In fact, as Christian contemplative masters have consistently observed from the Desert times right down into our own, without that critical intensity of ardor, it is all but impossible to escape the centrifugal force of human egotism. It takes gold to make gold; a heart that burns, even with carnal love, can be directed toward contemplation of higher things, but a heart of stone travels nowhere. As St. John Climacus observed with keen insight:

> I have seen impure souls who threw themselves headlong into physical *eros* to a frenzied degree. It was their very experience of that *eros* that led them to interior conversion. They concentrated their *eros* on the Lord. Rising above fear, they tried to love God with insatiable desire. That is why when Christ spoke to the woman who had been a sinner he did not say that she had been afraid, but that she had loved much, and had easily been able to surmount love by love.[14]

This goal of "surmounting love by love," or in other words, uniting the devotional and perceptive aspects of the heart in a single mystical flame, reveals the secret of why Christianity has always embraced affectivity as the gateway to inner awakening. We see this same predilection at work in *lectio divina*, where the third stage, *oratio*, is intended to take the concentrated attention of a mind that has gathered itself through *meditatio* and fan it to a level of emotional intensity wherein the boundaries of egoic consciousness are essentially melted, at least for the duration of the prayer. We see it again in the Jesus Prayer, classically understood, which while superficially resembling a mantra, in fact gains its force through the concentration of affective love.

This is also the underlying reason, I believe, that Christian tradition has never taken easily to meditation, and has never rested entirely comfortably with a methodology that seems to go against the grain of one of its most basic presuppositions: that it is not possible to reach the apophatic without first going through the cataphatic—i.e., via the concentration of affectivity. Working with *eros* as its transformational quicksilver, the journey necessarily entails a long, tough slog through the gristmills of purification and inner preparation before the soul is ready to "bear the beams of love" (in the words of William Blake) in pure contemplation. By an overwhelming majority, the pedagogy of both the Christian West and the Christian East has favored this developmental trajectory.

Attention of the heart
But majority is not the same thing as exclusive. While "concentration of affectivity" clearly dominates the field in Christian spirituality, there is also a different pathway to center, and one who was onto it was Simeon the New Theologian. His curiously little known essay, "Three Methods of Attention and Prayer," is one of the most important resources available for locating Centering Prayer within the wider tradition of Christian interior prayer and for validating its innovative yet entirely orthodox starting points.[15]

I have spoken of Simeon extensively in my book *Centering Prayer and Inner Awakening*, but let me briefly recap some of the essential points. Simeon was one of the most brilliant spiritual theologians of his day, or of any day. His lifespan (949–1022) places him almost exactly a thousand years ago, but the issues he was grappling with in the eleventh century are still cutting edge in our own times. Essentially, Simeon insisted on the dimension of *conscious presence* in our human relationship with the divine—or as he called it, "attention of the heart."

Developing this kind of attention is all-important, Simeon maintains, for otherwise, it is impossible to have purity of heart; impossible to fulfill the Beatitudes.[16] Only when the mind is "in the heart," grounded and tethered in that deeper wellspring of spiritual awareness, is it possible to live the teachings of Jesus without hypocrisy or burnout. The gospel requires a radical openness and compassion that is beyond the capacity of the anxious, fear-ridden ego.

But how to swim down to these deeper waters? Simeon lays out three possibilities. The first is the classic path of "concentration of affectivity" as we have just described it:

> If a man stands at prayer and, raising his hands, his eyes, and his mind to heaven, keeps in mind Divine thoughts, imagines celestial blessings, hierarchies of angels and dwellings of the saints, assembles briefly in his mind all he has learnt from the Holy Spirit and ponders over all this while at prayer, gazing up to heaven and thus inciting his soul to longing and love of God, at times even shedding tears and weeping, this will be the first method of prayer.[17]

The problem with this traditional method, Simeon asserts, is that it relies on a high level of excitement of the external faculties, which is ultimately self-delusional and can become addictive, leading one to depend on lights, sweet scents, and "other like phenomena" as evidence of the presence of God. "If then such a man give himself up to silence," Simeon adds bluntly, "he can scarcely avoid going out of his mind."[18]

The second method he explores is self-examination and the collecting of thoughts "so that they cease to wander"—the classic methodology of a practice based on awareness. This approach relies heavily on the practices of inner attention, self-remembering, and the examination of consciousness. But the fatal flaw in this methodology, Simeon observes, is that such a practitioner "remains in the head, whereas evil thoughts are generated in the heart."[19] In other words, the aspiring seeker is likely to be blindsided by the strength of his unconscious impulses.

Simeon designates the third method as *attention of the heart* and describes it as follows:

> You should observe three things before all else: freedom from all cares, not only cares about bad and vain but even about good things...your conscience should be clear so that it denounces you in nothing, and you should have a complete absence of passionate attachment, so that your thought inclines to nothing worldly.[20]

The importance of Simeon's observation here is extraordinary, for he has essentially described the practice of kenotic surrender. That greatest *desideratum* of the spiritual life, attention of the heart, is achieved, he feels, not so much by concentration of affectivity as by the simple release of all that one is clinging to, the good things as well as the bad things. He proposes that we start with that bare gesture of letting go. Attention of the heart can certainly be engaged through concentrated affectivity. But it can also, just as well, be engaged through relinquishing the passions and relaxing the will.

While Simeon is clearly describing an integrated practice combining both prayer and daily life, it is uncanny how closely his words dovetail with the basic methodology of Centering Prayer. As a person sits in Centering Prayer attempting to "resist no thought, retain no thought, react to no thought" (the instructional formula offered in all introductory training sessions), he or she is actually progressing in small but utterly real increments toward "freedom from all cares" and "the absence of passionate attachments." This is Simeon's "attention of the heart," which he states is inseparable from true prayer and true conversion. In fact, the case can be made that what Thomas Keating has really succeeded in doing is to give meditational form to Simeon's attention of the heart, thereby providing a powerful new access point to the traditional wisdom of the Christian inner path. His approach, like Simeon's, is innovative but entirely orthodox once you understand where he is coming from. The tie-in between Centering Prayer and Simeon's attention of the heart is simply another link in the chain situating Centering Prayer firmly within the lineage of Christian kenosis understood as spiritual path.

Finding the way to the heart

"Keep your mind there [in the heart]," remarks Simeon, "trying by every possible means to find the place where the heart is." In his *Lost Christianity*, Jacob Needleman immediately picks up on the irony of this: that as we begin, we do not know where the heart is. We must learn, through the process of repeated tuning in.[21]

My hunch is that this describes the actual journey of both Thomas Merton and Thomas Keating—and undoubtedly Simeon as well. During their respective monastic novitiates "the first method of attention and prayer" was what was available, and they each practiced it to its fullness. (And even in the early days of Centering Prayer teaching, the Sacred Word was initially described as a "love word": affectivity in capsule form, or in other words, an intense, concentrated version of "all those feelings known to man."[22] It was ultimately through the experience of contemplation itself that these spiritual masters came to their realization that all along it has been the surrender carrying them home.

In his inimitable way, Merton puts words to the barebones truth of this timeless moment: the "aha" realization that solves Simeon's (and Needleman's) koan of "the Way to the Heart:"

> This act of total surrender is not simply a fantastic intellectual and mystical gamble; it is something much more serious: it is an act of love for this unseen Person Who, in the very gift of love by which we surrender ourselves to His reality, also makes Himself present to us.[23]

If what he glimpses in this remarkable insight is true, then the response to those overly concerned that Centering Prayer is violating the traditional pedagogy can only be a gentle "All shall be well, and all manner of things shall be well." For ultimately, as this "unseen person" becomes present, the knee of the heart will instinctively bow—and the rest will somehow work itself out.

It is indeed true that ego-driven spiritual ambitiousness can wind up in very bad places. But it is important never to lose sight of the fact that *spiritual ambitiousness and attention of the heart are mutually exclusive categories.* The proud may fall, but it will not be through following the Way of the Heart, for the heart has its inbuilt safeguard: it perceives only in the modality of surrender (which means, literally, to "hand oneself over," to entrust oneself entirely). In other words, the heart can fulfill its function as organ of spiritual perception only to the degree that it is able to bring itself into moral alignment with "the infinity of love" (in Helminski's words); to the extent that it is willing and able to coincide with love, to become love itself. For love is the ultimate, and ultimately the *only,* purification. But this "Love which moves the sun and the stars" (as Dante calls it) is not a feeling, an *eros*-fixated-upon-God; it is rather the alchemical *agape* which comes into being when *eros* becomes whole in the act of giving itself away. Whenever and wherever along the pathway of prayer this great secret is learned, it instantaneously reorganizes the playing field.

Notes

1. Feldmeier, Peter, "Centering Prayer and the Christian Contemplative Tradition," *Spiritual Life* (Winter 2003), p. 239.
2. Steindl-Rast, David, "Man or Prayer," in Patrick Hart, ed., *Thomas Merton, Monk* (New York: Sheed & Ward, 1974), p. 90.
3. For more on this point, see my *Centering Prayer and Inner Awakening* (Cambridge, MA: Cowley Publications, 2004), Chapter 5: "Spiritual Non-Possessiveness."
4. Amis, Robin, ed., *Theophan the Recluse: Writings on Prayer of the Heart* (Newburyport, MA: Praxis Press, 1992), p. xx.
5. The word Islam itself means "submission"—i.e., the complete kenosis of self-emptying before God. For a brilliant and comprehensive study of Merton's late-life immersion in Sufism, see Baker, Rob and Gray Henry, eds., *Merton and Sufism: The Untold Story* (Louisville, KY: Fons Vitae, 1999).
6. Merton, Thomas, "A Member of the Human Race," *Conjectures of a Guilty Bystander* (New York: Doubleday, 1966, p. 158. Quoted from *A Thomas Merton Reader*, ed. Thomas P. McDonnell, rev. ed. (Garden City, NY: Image Books, 1974), pp. 346–7.
7. See Griffith, Sidney H., "Merton, Massignon, and the Challenge of Islam," in *Merton and Sufism*, pp. 64–5.
8. *Merton and Sufism*, p. 65.
9. Helmiski, Kabir, *Living Presence: A Sufi Way to Mindfulness and the Essential Self* (New York: Tarcher/Putnam, 1992), p. 157.
10. *Living Presence*, pp. 157–8.
11. Merton, Thomas, "True Freedom," transcribed by the author from the cassette series *Sufism: Longing for God* (Kansas City: Credence Cassettes, 1995).
12. *The Cloud of Unkowing*, ed. Ira Progoff (New York: Delta Books, 1957), p. 72.
13. Cassian, John, *Conferences*, trans. Colm Luibheid (Mahwah, NJ: Paulist Press, 1985), p. 133. Cassian's full explanation is as follows: "It carries within it a cry to God in the face of every danger. It expresses the humility of a pious confession. It conveys the watchfulness

born of unending worry and fear. It conveys sense of our frailty, the assurance of being heard, the confidence in help that is always and everywhere present."

14. Quoted from Cong, Joseph Chu, OCSO, *The Contemplative Experience* (New York: Crossroad, 1999), p. 27. This goal, in fact, comprises the basic pedagogy of monastic love mysticism, which has flowed like a great underground river through the spirituality of the Christian West, reaching its culmination in the writings of St. Bernard of Clairvaux. Chu Cong's book is a profound yet accessible introduction to this great tradition.

15. This essay is found in Kadloubovsky, E. and G. E. H. Palmer, eds., *Writings from the Philokalia on Prayer of the Heart* (London and Boston: Faber and Faber, 1951, 1992), pp. 152–61.

16. *Philokalia*, p. 158.

17. *Philokalia*, p. 153.

18. *Philokalia*, p. 153.

19. *Philokalia.*, p. 154. In this context the word "heart" obviously refers to what we would today call "the unconscious," a nuance unavailable to Simeon.

20. *Philokalia*, p. 158.

21. Needleman, Jacob, *Lost Christianity* (New York: Doubleday, 1980), p. x. The quotation from Simeon is from the *Philokalia*, p. 158.

22. This aspect of the Sacred Word has been consistently emphasized in the teachings of Father Basil Pennington. For further comments, see my Preface to Thomas Keating and Basil Pennington, *Finding Grace at the Center* (Woodstock VT: Skylight Paths, 2007).

23. Merton, Thomas, *The Inner Experience*, ed. William H. Shannon (San Francisco: HarperCollins, 2003), p. 44. The work was originally published as a series in several successive issues of *Cistercian Studies* in 1984 (vols. 18–19). My original introduction to this quotation was through a photocopy of one of these articles loaned to me by a monk of St. Benedict's Abbey, Snowmass, Colorado, in 1995; the quotation is found in the third article: 18: 3 (1983), p. 209.

THOMAS MERTON'S INCLUSIVITY AND ECUMENISM
Silencing the Gong and Cymbals

John Wu, Jr.

The Making of an Ecumenist

Passionate love of God and neighbor, and of learning, along with a prodigious gift of prophecy, appear to be unassailable signs of a saint. As a member of his religious community and correspondent to thousands, Thomas Merton as though unwittingly committed himself to the search for truth in a life of dialogue. His secret lay in that he did not regard other traditions as alien but integral to what he recognized as a unified human legacy that we all—without exception—rightfully share. In the preface to one of his books published abroad he wrote: "Man is made in the image of God, and until he is fully united with himself, with his brother, and with his God, the reign of God cannot come and manifest itself on earth so that all may see His Kingdom."[1] He recognized in the other unique qualities of knowledge and wisdom, and that, in inculcating and cultivating such qualities, he would become an ever more complete person, and closer to God. Goethe once wrote what can be applied to Merton: "Who is the happiest of men? He who values the merits of others, And in their pleasures takes joy, as though, 'twere his own.'"[2]

In coming upon other traditions, Merton brought himself ever more intimately into the inner sanctum of others and their cultures. He tread this path both through active learning and what might be called the Taoistic *wu wei*, literally "no action" or "non-action," or loosely rendered, "non-ado" or "action of the *Tao*." By the time Asian culture and thought had became more than a passing fancy for him, Merton was, through the concentrated mining of his own tradition, a master of both the active and contemplative ways of life. He was also abreast of their rich overtones and, equally, their limits. He understood the many pitfalls that belie activism, the dangers of meddling with both nature and the divine will; at the same time, he was equally observant of the dangers of contemplation degenerating into mere quietism, when one lives without a moral or spiritual compass. Monastic life taught him two critical lessons, one of earth, the other of heaven: the sacredness of labor and waiting expectantly and patiently for grace.

In *Entering the Silence*, the second volume of journals, Merton notes: "What God wants of me will crystallize out, and there are things I need badly to find out, but I know I cannot find them out by pushing and pulling."[3] From an Asian perspective, these words reflect the harmonization and reconciliation of Confucian humanism with Taoist contemplation. From his early twenties, Merton had already possessed the notion of life with harmony as both a given and intellectual virtue not so much to be pursued but as lived. In his prime when he threw himself fully into Asian philosophy, he was not coming upon virgin field, for much of what he was to learn then was an extension of what he already had in large measure.

In examining Merton's life, one wonders if before him there had ever been a writer who had taken *inclusivity*—believing intensely in and abiding by the oneness of humanity—more seriously than he, and was able to approach this with such naturalness and urgency. Paradoxically he did it by way of *exclusivity*. Perhaps it is not so paradoxical after all, for an ever more profound faith in his spiritual traditions led him as if straightaway into the waiting arms of other traditions. One might say that his brand of *inclusivity* might never have materialized had there not been a long period of mostly quiet incubation which then seemed to have exploded in him and led irresistibly outward toward a life of charity and generosity of spirit.

Looking back not to forty, but to well beyond seventy years, in the late 1930s when Merton was still a student at Columbia University, we see quite clearly that his future life already reflected a paradigm of what is possible in terms of dialogue when one possesses faith in a preexisting unity in life. Merton, like St. Benedict 1,500 years earlier, saw these seeds through the prism of others, but, at the same time, as a unity—*existentially broken*—that nevertheless begs to be mended. In its mending, this ultimately requires a *metanoia*, a radical "change of heart" among the struggling human family. Nothing seemed clearer to him, on the one hand, than the fact of human brokenness and our ineptness in fixing it, and, on the other, God's own desire, driven by a constancy of love, for humankind to return to Eden, not in some metaphorical, but *essential* way. It was no surprise then that in the work he saw for himself he was intrepid in soliciting the help of all traditions, or, at least those that maintain some original *natural untainted wholeness*. This he found in such philosophies as classical Confucianism, at least in that form undistorted by countless hegemonic agendas that have nearly torn out the very heart of the great Chinese Master and Teacher in its long, often agonizing 2,500-year history. Merton saw *wholeness* also in philosophical Taoism, in Sufism, the mystical arm of Islam, in the old Zen practitioners out to reform not only Buddhism but all forms of knowledge that have grown decrepit with words that no longer sit well with realities.

In these incursions, what is clear was the choice Merton made in emphasizing experience over potentially knotty theological questions and concerns, or, he recognized experience and theology as at least of being equal value, one supporting the other. Not only did he find a key to inter-religious dialogue in such thought—he saw them more as simple yet profound ways of life than thought or ideation—upon which he could imagine, perhaps ironic to many, finding the hidden regenerative roots for a revitalized future Christianity. He wanted to bring back to the table of humanity everything that was originally good as it comes from the hand of God. What underlined his thought throughout was the necessity of cultivating a clean or pure heart (*mundo corde*) that would reflect original goodness and without which no intellectual wizardry could bring true wisdom. This tendency made Merton at least partially Asian in the universal acknowledgment that "theory and practice are one," that one without the other would constitute a dangerous imbalance and, worse, a veritable aberration of life.

In Merton's writings intended to further interfaith dialogue and ecumenical concerns, he rarely indulges in academic exercises. Rather, he nearly always centered his efforts in relocating the source that he felt both existentially and which essentially held life and human existence together. Merton in the early days did not actually live such unity; yet his writings reflect the danger and dissatisfaction that go along with personal isolationism. In a preface he wrote for the Vietnamese translation of *No Man Is an Island*, he warns of the danger of being isolated: "When a man attempts to live by and for himself alone, he becomes a little 'island' of hate, greed, suspicion, fear, desire...All his judgments are affected by this untruth."[4]

Whether Merton actually succeeded as an ecumenist or not, the qualities which he demanded of himself with regard to his own tradition were a critical sense and a constant willingness to open oneself in order to facilitate acceptance of the other, not through condescension or fear, but in the belief that no matter what differences lay between traditions, there are universal links that will make dialogue not only possible but necessary and inevitable. As a Christian he took the Incarnation and Redemption with utmost seriousness and, I dare add, *joy*. In all of this, there was both great wisdom and genuine heroism to Merton's inquiry into truth. He took the following line from Psalm 33:11 literally: "They that seek the Lord shall not be deprived of any good." Like St. Paul, Merton learned well the critical lesson of a continuous dying to oneself in order to live an ever more complete life. We can see him applying this wisdom, among other places, in his dialogue with inter-faith friends. He saw in ecumenism a reconciliation of divisions, which basically meant, first of all, "healing the divisions in (ourselves)" so that we "could help heal the divisions of the whole world."[5]

We see this broad openness of spirit in his attentiveness to the Shakers, in a letter dated 1/24/62 to Mary Childs Black, in which he talks about "their deep significance, which manifests itself in a hidden and archetypal way in their art, craftsmanship, and in all their works." He saw in the Shaker "[as] perhaps the most authentic expression of the primitive American 'mystery' or 'myth': the paradise myth.... [N]ot just a return to the beginning, it is also an anticipation of the end. The anticipation of eschatological fulfillment, of completion, the New World was an earnest and a type of the New Spiritual Creation."[6]

Even as the Shakers as a community was coming to an end, Merton saw its charism as an "eschatological fulfillment," and, therefore, as a beginning, an encouragement not only for Christians but to everyone.

The way he saw the Shakers—and many other traditions—reflects the depth of a compassionate heart and the breadth of a cultivated mind that, over time, helped to train him to perceive all things, whether large or small, within a universal matrix. In words oft-cited in a letter from John C. H. Wu, my father struck a bull's-eye: "The beautiful thing about you is that your heart is as great as your mind. Thus in you love and knowledge are united organically. Herein lies your profound significance for this great age of synthesis of East and West."[7] He was a prophetic witness to the future because he had a clear sight of the present, and he did not allow himself to be fooled by things glittery and tawdry.

Merton's admonition of the necessity of seeing "our duty to mankind as a whole,"[8] vague and even innocuous on the surface, is significant and a difficult task to put into practice, for what the monk stresses ethically in a letter to James Forest, his young pacifist friend, was the moral duty of giving up all traces of *partisanship*, of avoiding the strong temptation to take sides, if one expects genuine harmony and peace among sensitive souls struggling to make precious headway in the then struggling peace movement.

It might have been people like Merton that C. S. Lewis had in mind when he said insightfully, "When God arrives (and only then) the half-gods can remain."[9] What is certain about this monk is that he was not writing on such critical issues as war and peace and preemptive nuclear strike merely as intellectual exercise nor consciously pushing a particular political or social agenda. Having seen the rise of totalitarian regimes, he lived through precarious times. As Hannah Arendt and others knew so well, writers at such times put words to paper to save oneself and society, including its culture and civilization. As a committed ecumenist, Merton found in love and compassion a moral and spiritual platform upon which to stand with others. Like Confucius (551-479 BCE) who lived in equally "dark times," the Period of the Warring States, Merton sought a recovery and, therefore, a re-discovery of interior, God-given qualities so much needed to dispel the moral blight that invades and desecrates human lives and existence. Without such a recovery, no moral reconstruction would be possible.

In reading Merton, one is often struck that his writings, though for and to others, come constitutionally in the form of cautionary warnings and admonitions to *himself*. This is consistent with his journals and his self-estimation as basically an existentialist. Merton and Albert Camus, whom he loved and with whom he identified, therefore, remind us of the classical Asian approach toward ideas, principally as found in Wang Yang-ming (1472-1529), the great Neo-Confucian philosopher whose writings and life show strong strains of the mystical. One principal idea in both the *Confucian Analects* and the *Mencius* was *cheng-ming*, conventionally rendered as "rectification of names." According to this principle, the sacred task of each person is to fulfill to the best of one's ability what one's role in life demands. Perhaps it was from this ancient, ever profitable principle that is derived one of the centerpieces of Wang Yang-ming's thought, that is, the principle that goes by the well-known notion of *chih-hsing-ho-i*, that is, "theory and practice are fundamentally one," or, "the inseparability of knowledge and action." Much can be made of Merton's own idea of "contemplative action," which is beyond the scope of this essay. One can clearly see what Merton was driving at: the necessity of uniting action with what is deepest in each of us, a contemplative vision based on love and compassion.

The greatness of the ancients is that they took both theory and practice seriously. They understood the critical nature of reconciling the two as an initial step in the restoration and restructuring of both self and society. Confucius, Mencius and Wang Yang-ming, on the one hand, and Camus, Merton and even Herbert Marcuse, the neo-Marxist, on the other, all grasped well the significance of words, and how their use can make or break society. Both the recovery of the person and of society demands that we critically recognize not only the importance of words but how words can structure the very nature of our reality. Merton untiringly warned us of the dangers of political propaganda and the onus of advertising that in our relatively new century has reached alarming proportions.

In a journal entry dated April 29, 1940, a year and a half before entering Gethsemani, he wrote of a seemingly simple yet extraordinary experience he had at the Church of St. Francis in Havana (or Camaguay, for it is not specified) as he witnessed children fervently reciting the Credo in Spanish. I mention this only because my father's words of praise for his friend regarding his mind and heart profoundly resonate with the way the future monk responded to the wholly spontaneous and naïve manner in which the Cuban children prayed the Credo. Obviously moved, Merton's response, inspired and prophetic, presages his future inter-religious work: "And so the unshakeable certainty, the clear and immediate knowledge that heaven was right in front of me, struck me like a thunderbolt and went through me like a flash of lightning and seemed to lift me clear up off the earth."[10] The tone is so reflective of the celebratory words that frame his joy in his descriptions of having experienced the oneness of humanity on the corner of Fourth and Walnut in Louisville and, shortly before his fateful passing, among the giant stone Buddhas at Polunnaruwa in the then Ceylon during his fateful Asian journey. The above words would be enough, but Merton goes on to add a further dimension. The experience of apprehending

> ...God in all His essence, all His power, God in the flesh and God in Himself...was not just the apprehension of a reality, of a truth, but at the same time and equally *a strong movement of delight, a great delight, like a great shout of joy and...it was as much an experience of loving as of knowing something, and in it love and knowledge were completely inseparable.*[11] (my emphasis)

Merton then expresses the overflowing spiritual gladness that follows his certitude of faith and the joy that is universally felt. Of these things, he is convinced, "there is nothing esoteric...and they happen to everybody, absolutely everybody, in some degree or other. These moments of God's grace are peculiar to nobody, but they stir in everybody, for it is by them that God calls people to Him, and He calls everybody... They are common to every creature that was ever born with a soul."[12] The words here appear somewhat tangled, even prosaic and scholastic, but the feelings run so very deep.

A universal humanity

Seeing things through a universal prism aided Merton in freeing himself from a ghetto mentality he knew plagued even his fellow believers. Perhaps that is one reason he grew to need so much communication with others, as a way to prevent the scourge of pride that isolation may sometimes foster. In his journals, we often come across complaints of his having to answer the usual backlog of letters. Yet, to the very end, he seemed to have regarded letter-writing with a good deal of patience and charity, just as a Confucian might have done in fulfillment of a moral duty. In a previously cited letter to Forest, we saw Merton remonstrating with and gently giving warning to his sometimes impetuous young friend. He suggests that workers for peace need to cultivate and understand a "deep patient compassion for the fears of men (sic), for the fears and irrational mania of those who hate us or condemn us."[13]

Merton's appeal lay in his ability to challenge others—irrespective of the tradition they originally belonged—into becoming increasingly more universal. One feels he was only capable of living within a universal framework. This forging of unity was irresistible to him, it being his *modus operandi*, and therefore something natural. Perhaps beginning initially as a reflex, it gradually became a cultivated habit driven by a love seeking ever greater fulfillment the further he found others seeking similar fulfillment. His correspondence, literally *to the world*, was an extension of his love and concern for his own Cistersian brotherhood. In fact, one could easily perceive his ecumenism to be an after-thought, shall we say, a natural development of his innate love for learning not so much reflective of a *learned* person but of one unceasingly *learning*. This was what Confucius himself wanted most to be remembered for, as someone who was untiring in his love for learning. Like Confucius, there was both an intellectual and spiritual side to Merton that enlarged and gave considerable ballast to his moral being, a ceaseless cultivation of mind along with heart that prevents any of us from becoming moral prigs.

Merton struggled mightily to overcome his limitations through solitude and prayer that helped to discipline what he saw in himself as in possession of a willful mind, which he needed constantly to renounce. Serious as his intent was, the monk's relationship with God was of such intimacy that it was characterized by both a playfulness and sense of levity one finds in Chuang Tzu and scattered throughout Zen and Taoist literature. It is also a quality that seasons and gives great disarming charm to the letters between the monk and my father. This, plus the shared realization that what little wisdom they possessed, would be even far less had they not realized how poor their lives would be without being guided by grace: they seldom failed to understand the distinction between "playing God" and "letting God play." Both conversions seemed based on the recovery of Eden and the inexplicable joy that goes along with it.[14] Childlike playfulness is what *both* Merton and Wu saw. They found it most appealing in such Asian literatures and therefore also what they most wanted to return to Christianity as a way of revitalizing its aching, decaying bones. In a sense, love of learning, then, was truly love of *unlearning* in which, directed by grace, we understand learning not as the sometimes harmful accumulation of knowledge but rather the renunciation or casting off of excess baggage that prevents our being from taking wing. Typically, as if working with a two-edged sword, in wanting to revitalize their own respective traditions, they both gave life back to other traditions. This is the clearest indication that their method radically contrasted with that of "triumphalist" Christianity. It is uncanny how much and how deeply these two men reflected one another, nor should we be surprised that they were converts—out to bring light into the dark times in which they flourished. The following prayer—one could choose any from among hundreds that enrich his early journals and spiritual writings—summarizes not only Merton's very own charism but that of any Christian of a contemplative, mystical strain: "My God, lock me in Your Will, imprison me in Your Love and Your wisdom, draw me to Yourself. I will never do anything when the strongest reason for doing it is only my own satisfaction."[15]

Merton's prayers reflect the strong thirst for grace to enter God's will. The words, "I will never do anything when the strongest reason for doing it is only my own satisfaction," are surely uncharacteristic of one so much in love with learning. Merton makes the presence of God a common practice, without which would make life absurd; in doing so, he avoids the prideful temptation of satisfying mere urges rooted in narcissism. The practice of divine presence led him back not only to God's children but to all authentic traditions marked by the presence of the Holy.

Wisdom in Merton lay in his understanding of proportionality, of balance, of the critical difference between the natural and the transcendent, of human willfulness and following the divine will.

In his spiritual writings Merton shares with us the wisdom of the Psalter. The daily chanting of the Psalms in his monastery guided him and his brother monks and, in listening attentively to its content, there seems to be no greater message of balance or harmony to be found, neither in Confucianism nor in Taoism, whose trademark is tranquility and bliss. To be sure, we also find them in the Psalms, but the latter also taught him to work through struggle and conflict, to strive for ever greater depth and clarity. His writings, particularly in the 1960s and the collection famously known as *The Cold War Letters* are therefore a powerful explosion of the kind of righteous anger—of a continuous casting forth of jeremiads—one finds in the Psalms and among the Old Testament prophets. A cursory reading of those urgent missives clearly indicates that Merton's concerns did not stop with the single moral question of pre-emptive nuclear strike but with dozens of other significant issues.

Both the secular and divine drama—mostly hidden—is altogether so personal and universal that one need not be a Christian to appreciate and participate in it. One needs only to acknowledge one's full humanity in order to *share* Merton's multi-levels of reality.

It was because he was deeply rooted as a servant of God so committed to his vocation and his Church that, even if one disagrees with his politics, one finds it difficult to question the motive or authenticity of what he believed in. His was nothing less than a voice in the twentieth century wilderness, a voice containing all the righteous anguish of an old Jewish prophet or a John the Baptist without shame aiming to right the wrongs of a society that had forgotten God's covenant, that his words represented nothing less than an outrage over a world gone mad.

In the mid-1990s, on one of two occasions I had the enormous pleasure of meeting James Laughlin at his home in Norfolk, Connecticut. The New Directions founder and publisher and Merton's great friend mentioned his staff being overwhelmed by both the quantity and quality of Merton's non-stop output. The octogenarian at one point simply exclaimed, "We had no idea where all the stuff was coming from and when he found the time to write, and he always sent such fine things, too!" In retrospect, one can only conclude that Merton's vast output could only have been attributed to his obsession for truth, and, in the case of the *Cold War Letters*, he was indeed a strong solitary voice desperately trying to bring order out of disorder.

Merton's love of learning included tasting whatever God had touched and brought to life by all those that the Maker, in His pure wisdom and total freedom, had chosen to leave to humankind. In a sense, Merton is the Christian *bodhisattva* so in love with God, neighbor and creation that he cannot imagine himself savoring heaven without both his friends and enemies there with him.

In his introduction to *Dialogues with Silence*, Jonathan Montaldo says insightfully, "who Merton really was in all his complexity must ultimately remain a mystery." In a wonderful visual image Montaldo compares the monk to "a still life of a bird in flight," but that "no matter how beautiful and true to the color of the creature's wings, (it) does not reveal how the bird actually flew. A photograph catches only one frame, not the full trajectory of the flight itself."[16]

Merton's most inspired words—particularly his prayers—remind us of the ancients who knew better than we the dire poverty of verbal formulations. They understood implicitly the inseparability of knowledge and virtue. For, being solidly grounded in the here and now and, in their wisdom in which they viewed life organically, they took for granted the relationship between heaven and earth and were open to wherever and whatever the Divine would wish to take and make of them.

Merton rarely allowed the philosophical and the scholastic theologian in him to override the existential poet and contemplative priest. Despite writing voluminously, it is astonishing how little he was tempted to give final names to things, for he seemed to have mastered the immortal first line of Lao Tzu's *Tao Teh Ching*: "The tao that can be talked about is not the Eternal *Tao*," which is Nameless, "Mystery of mysteries" and "Door of all essence."[17]

From daily involvement with Holy Scripture and later the ancient wisdom of Asia, he happened upon the essential lesson that constitutes ancient learning: all genuine learning, guided by the *Tao*, begins, as we have mentioned above, with *unlearning*: "Learning consists in daily accumulating,/ The practice of *Tao* consists in daily diminishing."[18] Without this initial piety, all learning becomes misdirected the moment the mind directs itself to knowledge that, rather than enlighten, tampers with what ought to be left alone. Merton had no need to go very far for this essential lesson; it lay in the very wisdom that one finds in the Beatitudes, or in any of the righteous warnings of the Psalter.

Chapter 20 of the *Tao Teh Ching* best summarizes some of Merton's essential qualities of mind and heart. If we regard the words paradoxically, as if through a Taoist palimpsest, we could easily imagine the monk speaking through *Lao-Chuang*. Here, it is Lao Tzu saying his own

Yes not so much to existence but to life's essence and the Eternal *Tao* that, perhaps, guards the very gate of Eden: "Have done with learning,/ And you will have no vexation./How great is the difference between 'eh' and 'o'?/What is the distinction between 'good' and 'evil'?/…. All men settle down in their grooves:/I alone am stubborn and remain outside./ But wherein I am most different from others is/In knowing to take sustenance from my Mother!" If *grace* is not exactly what the Taoist had in mind, he certainly came close to it: "To take sustenance from my Mother" is to "spring beyond the world."[19]

In the last stanza, Lao Tzu contrasts the self-willed individual with himself, one who understands from whence life springs. Although these insightful, paradoxical words were uttered some 2,500 years ago in a remote land by one never seen again, the lessons therein may be far more relevant to us now than they were then. Ironically, to "remain outside" and to be in no grooves is to find oneself squarely in the very center of life.

Whatever else universality might mean, Merton knew instinctively no interfaith dialogue or ecumenistic agendas could survive for long without a solid foundation in shared authentic experiences that reflect the strong craving for universal truth. Merton sought after learning that pointed to the simple heart of the person able to dispense with complex diversions of life that, rather freeing the soul, keeps it in chains. One can well imagine how Lao Tzu's playful verses could serve as a complement to the *Rule* of St. Benedict, each giving insight and new life to the other.

What stands out in Wu's translation of the *Tao Teh Ching* is its childlike playfulness and idiomatic phrases that catch the spirit of Lao Tzu in the same way Merton so well caught the spirit of Chuang Tzu; what one does not want in a translation is some stuffy, academic fare; hence any rendering has to be simple, even naïve, filled with earthy wisdom and a joyfulness reflecting the "*Tao* that cannot be talked about" and the Holy Spirit and our eternal kinship with it. The ideal for *Lao-Chuang* as it is for the Trinity is that the only speech adequate for us are words "spoken in tongues," in language that transcends language that, in being spoken, explodes its very structure and reveals its inner Source, the voice of the Holy that by happenstance we adopt as our own voice.

One way of seeing Merton's idea of ecumenism: surely not as an abstract, formalized theological formula, but within the framework of a universal human endeavor indispensable for the physical and spiritual preservation and survival of the earth. In deference to others, he never presented to anyone a completed package of what he expected from the other; he chose rather to give himself to others the *fragmented life of a stranger*. It can be said, to understand Merton—as many have pointed out—is to identify with the marginalized. Because he genuinely believed he did not "know where his life was going," which is not so much a humble admission of some personal flaw but the very condition—Montaldo says, the monk's continual, never-ending journey "to love learning and desire God," to me the very moorings of his fertile life—that makes dialogue not only possible but inevitable.

As time went on, the shades of the triumphalist Merton found in earlier writings, receded. He became conscious of the potential evils of condescension. He took the time to extensively rewrite Seeds of Contemplation, the original of which was considered a modern classic. Perhaps it was because his faith had grown strong there was no longer any necessity of striking even the slightest defensive pose. Humility and deference toward others, for millennia the signature of ancient Asian culture, particularly as applied to Confucian ethics, solidly served to anchor Merton's ever-growing faith. If we are watchful in keeping Confucian ethics from degenerating into a narrow system of ethics that becomes a plaything for a political state pursuing dominance and hegemonic ends, one sees in it *a gentleness of mind and heart*—not an obsequious docility—born of a sweetness from which is derived genuine inner strength. Obviously, such gentleness has deep spiritual resonances. Merton saw this meekness in both Confucianism and Taoism as a paradoxical and hidden efficacy that so well complements the Gospels.

Although Jonathan Montaldo's wise assessment centers on Merton's interior growth as seen in his prayerful life and art—clearly central to his vocation—we may perhaps appropriate his words in attempting to understand how it was not only possible but became the monk's own original way of presenting himself to the other as a way to pave a path to a more expansive understanding of whatever wisdom tradition he was trying to unlock and assimilate. Montaldo provides two important ideas in Merton: *"ignorance acknowledged"* and *"darkness acknowledged"*:

"Ignorance acknowledged was a stimulus to new experience..., an exciting wisdom that poised Merton for God's 'next thing.' Darkness acknowledged kept Merton leaning toward the 'thin places' between night and the edge of light that signals dawn," (keeping) "him sober and watchful...so that he might not miss a gate to the rose garden or pass a door that might lead to paradise and deliverance from the cycle of loss and recovery and loss again."[20] It is this uniquely Mertonian humility that is so well reflected in the famous prayer beginning, "My Lord God, I have no idea where I am going."[21]

Dying in order to Live

In "Learning to Live," on the surface, a short, whimsical essay, but in fact a remarkable piece of writing he wrote in dead earnest in response to a request from Columbia University, which had selected him as a distinguished alumnus, Merton wrote: "One graduates by rising from the dead. Learning to be oneself means, therefore, learning to die in order to live." To Merton, as it certainly would have been true for Lao Tzu if we but trust the spirit of his words, education meant far more than being learned or, worse, the mere accumulation of knowledge. It meant to the monk, "discovering in the ground of one's being a 'self' which is ultimate and indestructible, which not only survives the destruction of all other more superficial selves but finds its identity affirmed and clarified by their destruction."[22] The lessons Merton attempts to instill are far-reaching and deeply philosophical. What education should not aim at, says Merton, is "to impose a prefabricated definition of the world," which would result in totally falsifying both the self and the world. He goes on: "The function of a university" is not only "to help the student to discover himself...and to identify who it is that chooses," but primarily "to help men and women save their souls and, in so doing, to save their society: from what? From the hell of meaninglessness, of obsession, of systematic lying, of criminal evasions and neglects, of self-destructive futilities."[23]

If we view ecumenism within the context of how Merton sees the purpose of education, then ecumenism is not a set goal but a continual process, to grow into authenticity by allowing ourselves to become as universal as God wishes us to be in His plan for human unity. Although "Learning to Live" addresses a largely well-educated, secular audience,

Merton did not hesitate to use religious language when he wished to make a salient point: "Speaking as a Christian existentialist, I mean by 'soul' not simply the Aristotelian essential form but the mature personal identity, the creative fruit of an authentic and lucid search, the 'self' that is found after other partial and exterior selves have been discarded as masks."[24] He then naturally segues into what the Taoists would surely have approved: "This metaphor must not mislead: this inner identity is not 'found' as an object, but is the very self that finds. It is lost when it forgets to find, when it does not know how to seek, or when it seeks itself as an object…Hence the paradox that it finds best when it stops seeking."[25]

These words are a perfect paraphrase for *Taoistic non-action*, the spontaneous carrying out of all affairs without ado and in total detachment and self-abandonment, in which one is not driven obsessively by results or questions of success and failure. When one learns to stop seeking, "one no longer seeks to be told by another who one is."[26] At this point authentic dialogue finally becomes possible as everything then falls within the realm of possibility. This has subtle, far-reaching implications not only in terms of conventional interpersonal relationships but for establishing a broad basis for healthy, fruitful dialogue among men and women of diverse religious communions and persuasions.

Whether viewed religiously or secularly, the idea of dying in order to live has a powerful meaning. Although appearing simple, it is a difficult goal for, whether we are teachers or students, old or young, as creatures of habit we are apt to fall back into ways we have been raised and find ourselves most comfortable settling into. Besides, we need to be at least somewhat enlightened enough to understand this admonition of *dying in order to live*. To the Taoist, it was as simple as that; to those bred in the West, we have been excessively filled with words and multifarious theories that often trap rather than liberate.

As for present-day Asia, we have done all we can to try to outstrip the West in every way without hardly an inkling of suspicion that we have enmeshed ourselves in ways that perhaps drive us into greater alienation than the West has ever known. Reason? Because in some cases we have abandoned our cultures and traditions far more blatantly than the West has cast away theirs.

JOHN WU, JR.

Merton had one foot in Eden, but he was no dreamer. He was a contemporary universalist who had no illusions as to what was happening to cultures worldwide; nor was he romancing any particular present-day culture which he knew was either on this or that side of *cargo*, and that no *cargo*, either the giving or the taking of it, was a solution to its inbred emptiness and unhappiness. Here he was echoing Mahatma Gandhi who had the great wisdom to know the unhappiness that the West was exporting to the rest of the world. The exportation continues at a far more alarming rate than either Gandhi or Merton thought possible. The contemporary craving for material possessions has grown exponentially, and the stronger the craving, the deeper the alienation and the more neurotically restless we find ourselves.

The fundamental question that haunts us is: what exactly constitutes wisdom in an age of unprecedented technological innovations and fashions that find their demise the moment they hit the market? Merton himself remains a cultural paradigm for he was able to embody, as we suggested in the beginning, the best in his own traditions and, as the decades unfolded, the best that he found in those of others. The renaissance we find in his rich life and writings are not a mere collection of unrelated and scattered cultural items but a unified vision based on profound learning that he shared with others, all of which was motivated by the ultimate desire for the Face of God. The lesson we learn is the necessity to undergo a radical re-education in order to regain the basic roots of life that we have such trouble locating.

Merton's signal warnings go back at least to the earliest Hebraic Scriptures as well as Chinese writings of yore, and including all the earthy wisdom traditions, oral and written. There are obvious reasons why Lao Tzu and Chuang Tzu, the Taoist giants, will continue to attract our attention and why Confucianism is seen once again rearing its proverbial head even in a present-day China that remains authoritarian.

Let me here once more solicit the aid of the last stanza in Chapter 20 of the *Tao Teh Ching* beginning with "All men settle down in their grooves." Our idea of self-discovery can often mean identifying the self with that particular niche or goal we have attained. Even in our spiritual life we may find ourselves comfortably enslaved by that one fine cranny that we inadvertently let determine who and what we are. To "find the self" can often mean identifying the self with that particular niche or goal. To the Taoists as well as Merton, the preservation of the authentic self is, paradoxically, to "remain outside" all grooves or, the way the monk might see it, to be *marginalized as a stranger*, to which Merton fully identified.

Ralph Waldo Emerson was probably unknowing even to himself a true Taoist, even more so than his friend, Thoreau, though a great nature lover but not a true contemplative. At least, this was the estimation of my father and Lin Yu-tang, both of whom wrote on and did exceptional translations of the *Tao Teh Ching*. Dr. Lin, in fact, states rather humbly that without inspiration from several of Emerson's essays, he could not have completed either that difficult work or the splendid selected portions from Chuang Tzu that illuminate each chapter of his renderings of the Laotsean classic. Emerson is at his purest and most profound in this mystical rhapsody from "Circles." If we listen closely we will hear not only *Lao-Chuang* but also Merton the Trappist:

> There is no virtue that is final; all are initial. The virtues of society are vices of the saint...Do not set the least value on what I do, or the least discredit on what I do not, as if I pretended to settle anything as true or false. I unsettle all things. No facts are to me sacred; none are profane; I simply experiment, an endless seeker with no Past at my back...Whilst the eternal generation of circles proceeds, the eternal generator abides...*People wish to be settled; only as far as they are unsettled is there any hope for them.*[27] (my emphasis)

Rather than being driven by the *source of life* to which we enter by *dying to ourselves*, we dig ourselves ever deeper into crannies and grooves that either others or we have dug without rhyme or reason. It would seem only a radical reversal of values would do to right things that appear to have gone askew.

What has become clear and, I think, a great boon to us lay folk, is that Merton did not merely write for his fellow monks and religious; he wrote—even in his earliest writings—for a world that continues to be held tenuously together by ideas that clip our wings and undermine the purpose of existence. For centuries we have been overwhelmed by ideas that reflect *functionality*—that is, of what "works"—that cannot inform us as to what we ought to do in order to bring genuine richness into our lives. As the French social philosopher Jacques Ellul might say, to let technic or technology dominate and determine so many aspects of our lives is an extraordinary loss. We are, most of us, thoroughly unsuited to live globally for we are far from that consciousness required of us to live in peaceful tranquility. Merton would say that we have not yet sufficiently died to ourselves to make such living possible.

At the end of "A Note to the Reader" in *The Way of Chuang Tzu*, Merton gives us an insight into the possible connection between the Taoist and the Crucified and Resurrected Christ. He says,

> For Chuang Tzu, as for the Gospel, to lose one's life is to save it, and to seek to save it for one's own sake is to lose it. There is an affirmation of the world that is nothing but ruin and loss. There is a renunciation of the world that finds and saves man (sic) in his own home, which is God's world...Chuang Tzu would have agreed with St. John of the Cross, that you enter upon this kind of a way when you leave all ways and, in some sense, get lost.[28]

Ecumenism of a *stranger*

Why would anyone regard *Day of a Stranger* ecumenical? Even in Merton's earliest writings, the reader finds him reaching for new horizons, expanding the possibilities of religion, of religious consciousness or, as a semi-hermit, falling in love with physical nature and entertaining ideas that are deeply human in order to sacramentalize daily existence. To Merton, nothing was anything if not centered upon ritual and rite, that is, the act and process of recovering the reverential in life so that the sacred becomes naturally linked to the secular.

The essay begs the large question: "What is the sense and use of religion and religious consciousness when we are unable to share what is most basic and ordinary, that is, people, nature and things that we find also the most intimate in our lives?" "Day of a Stranger" is writing that Chuang Tzu himself would have taken pride in: "a sermon to the everyday." In this essay that has the feel of *pure breath*, Merton helps us to see what is already there before us, a vision that approximates Eden. With clarity we see all the dimensionalities of existence take on the fullness of ever-renewed life. Wherever he goes—to the

Psalms that bring us to God and His creation, to nature that reflects its Creator, to the everyday use of ordinary things—Merton seems incapable of not stretching their meaning merely through his *attentiveness* to them, when the actor and the performance is one and the same, when the One playing is Someone infinitely greater than himself. He discovers in its unity a joyous fecundity, richness that is of the earth, yet far more, and in giving them a contemporary setting, they, as it were, gain life immeasurably.

The *usefulness of the useless* is paramount to the understanding of *Lao-Chuang*, who took the misnamed *useless* to transcendent heights and without which we would be spiritually indigent and languishing in some nightmarishly functional, colonized world with no way out. Even if the cargo comes in great abundance, it does not add an iota to *who I am, the blessed self*. Or, we, in borrowing Merton's words, eyes and ears, see and hear in ways that are no longer foreign, no longer alienating. How wondrous in such an ordinary day, he shows—*without showing*—how to live close to the flesh, to bridge that wounded brokenness that separates us from ourselves and the rest of creation in a niche—his hermitage, the only earthly home he could claim his own—which, because given by the Creator, has a manifestly universal *feel* to it.

So much of his writings, art, *calligraphs* and photographs, emanating naturally from deep spiritual springs serve as means to transport us closer to that promised life. They are as sacred as the liturgical cycle used in some Christian churches, and remind us of what we take for granted, each item a gift from the Godhead for our sanctification. To Merton, the more absorbed he was in his own daily liturgy—beginning with the Mass he loved so well—the greater feeling he had for the simplicity for such folks as the Shakers at Pleasant Hill.

It is also little wonder that he felt connected to the purity and simplicity of the Zen adepts, and "surrounded by all the silent Tzu's and Fu's (men without office and without obligation)"[29] for they too were to the square world strangers who, some defying even simple technology, refused to be absorbed into mechanized society.

In a letter to Czeslaw Milosz, Merton said those in the West could not avoid the obsession of always "counting, counting, counting!" This does not merely include numbers but the numbing bombardment of information—largely unfiltered and indigestible—that attacks us unabated. This obsession with *counting* or quantification has become appropriated by a high-tech East since Merton's passing. Now the reversal seems true: Asians now take pride in the mass hoarding of material life and its new religion lies partly in the interest many have in the complete "makeover" of physical attractiveness driven by a collective narcissism; many would find it "bad taste" to discuss what constitutes quality or the moral or spiritual life except when mixed with large doses of material life, which has become a quintessential concern.

Notes

1. Merton, Thomas, *"Honorable Reader": Reflections of My Work*, ed. Robert E. Daggy (New York: Crossroad Publishing Co., 1989), p. 43.
2. Wu, John C. H., *Joy in Chinese Philosophy* (Taipei, Taiwan: Wisdom Press, 1999), p. 14.
3. Merton, Thomas, *Entering the Silence: The Journals of Thomas Merton*, ed. Jonathan Montaldo (San Francisco: HarperCollins, 1996), p. 139.
4. Merton, Thomas, *"Honorable Reader,"* p. 126.
5. Ibid., p. 86.
6. Merton, Thomas, *Cold War Letters*, ed. Christine M. Bochen and William H. Shannon (Maryknoll, NY: Orbis Books, 2006) #24a, pp. 55-6.
7. *Wu-Merton Letters*, Wu to Merton, 9/6/1966 (unpublished).
8. Merton, Thomas, *Cold War Letters*, #25, p. 58.
9. Lewis, C. S., *The Four Loves* (Glasgow: William Collins Sons and Co., 1960), p. 109.
10. Merton, Thomas, *Run to the Mountain: The Journals of Thomas Merton*, ed. Patrick Hart (San Francisco: HarperSan Francisco, 1995), p. 218.
11. Ibid.
12. Ibid.
13. Merton, Thomas, *Cold War Letters*, #25.
14. See Wu, John, Jr., "A Lovely Day for a Friendship: The Spiritual and Intellectual Relationship Between Thomas Merton and John Wu As Suggested in Their Correspondence," in *The Merton Annual*, ed. Robert E. Daggy, et al, Vol. 5 (New York: AMS Press, 1997), pp. 311-54.
15. Thomas Merton, *Dialogues with Silence*, ed. Jonathan Montaldo (San Francisco: HarperCollins, 2001), p. 43. Originally, *Entering the Silence*, pp. 101-2.
16. Merton, *Dialogues with Silence*, p. xv.
17. See Tzu, Lao, *Tao The Ching*, trans. John C. H. Wu (Boston and London: Shambhala Press, 1989), chap. 1.
18. Ibid., chapter 48.
19. In a letter dated 1/10/66, my father, palpably lonely, wrote to Merton the following four-line poem, which he called a haiku: "Silent Lamp! Silent Lamp!/ I see only its radiance/ But hear not its voice!/ Spring beyond the world!" In an earlier letter (12/17/65), my father had sent a Chinese calligraphy which he dedicated to "Mei Teng," meaning "Silent Lamp." Merton replied on 12/28/65: "So it was moving to be 'baptized' in Chinese with a name

I must live up to. After all, a name indicates a divine demand. Hence I must be Mei Teng, a silent lamp, not a sputtering one."

20. Merton, Thomas, *Dialogues with Silence*, pp. xiv-xv.
21. Ibid., p. vii.
22. Merton, Thomas, "Learning to Live" in *Love and Living*, ed. Naomi Burton Stone and Patrick Hart (New York: Farrar, Straus and Giroux, 1980), p. 5.
23. Ibid., p. 4.
24. Ibid.
25. Ibid.
26. Ibid.
27. See "Circles," *The Complete Writings of R.W. Emerson* (New York: Wm. H. Wise and Co., 1929), pp. 221-2.
28. Merton, Thomas, "A Note to the Reader," in *The Way of Chuang Tzu* (New York: New Directions, 1965), pp. xv-xvi.
29. Merton, Thomas, *Day of a Stranger* (Salt Lake City, UT: Gibbs M. Smith, Inc., 1981), p. 63.

GOING EAST WITH MERTON
Forty Years Later—And Coming West with
Paramahansa Yogananda Today

Emile J. Farge

Parallels

As the plane bearing him to Asia lifted off in October of 1968, Thomas Merton entered into his journal "I with Christian mantras and a great sense of destiny...may I not come back without having settled the great affair...I am going home, to the home where I have never been in this body."[1] The "great affair" was his need to deepen the mysterious thoughts, feelings, prayerful yearnings, as well as the theological implications which seemed to be common to more and more students of religion as the twentieth century unfolded. He sought a deeper understanding of the *sameness versus the differences* between the fundamental Eastern and Western concepts of God and man's relatedness to him/her. This article examines parallels in Merton's life-work with a remarkable mystic.

Long before this final journey Thomas Merton had been engaged as a student of Buddhism (for some years, primarily in the Zen tradition), yet also of Hinduism and Gandhi, as well as several distinct Christian traditions other than his Roman Catholic faith to which he converted at age twenty-three. His first journey out of the monastery and back to New York City was in 1964, after twenty-three years of being cloistered. He went to New York to spend a few hours with Daisetz Suzuki as the Zen scholar was visiting there.[2] It had become quite clear to Merton that no one religious tradition should dare to monopolize the entirety of humankind's ability to relate to his creator, sustainer, and intimate lover. Indeed the 1968 journey to Asia, then twenty-seven years since entering a Cistercian monastery, seemed to deepen Merton's long-held notion that East and West have a great deal to teach each other and to learn from the other. After eight intensive weeks of visiting Buddhist and Hindu masters, Merton's urgency for more interplay among religious traditions would become still more compelling. He had prepared a talk he was to give in Calcutta. This was not to take place. Thomas Merton died on December 10, 1968 from a tragic accident with a faulty electric fan.[3] He had written that one can remain quite Christian while learning intimately from Buddhist or Hindu masters, adding "…I believe that some of us need to do this in order to improve the quality of our own…life and even help in the task of…renewal."[4]

Another planned encounter on his unfulfilled itinerary was to meet with Bede Griffiths, a Benedictine monk who had lived for thirty-five years in an Indian ashram. In that place Griffiths (aka Swami Dayananda—bliss of compassion) was a lone Catholic among the God-seekers from various religious traditions, being enriched by his colleagues, the Hindu environment and his own Roman Catholic tradition. We are today deprived of the possible content of the meeting between the two that was never held.[5]

In an earlier article published in *The Merton Annual*, I analyzed the similarities in the understanding of several key teachings of Christ and Christian living as taught by the Cistercian Father Louis (known to the world as Thomas Merton) and the Hindu Master, Paramahansa Yogananda.[6] Both men were born and educated on another continent (France/England for Merton, and India for Yogananda); both came to the United States and stayed thirty-two years after their arrival until their death. Both had their autobiographies published in the post-WWII 1940s, and both of those autobiographies are classics.[7] Both died before reaching age sixty. Despite so many similarities the two spiritual masters did not, to the best of our knowledge, read the other's offerings or ever quote the other.

Followers of Merton have established an international organization (The International Thomas Merton Society) to mine, publish and propagate his writings and spiritual teachings. The society both monitors the spreading world impact of this modern God seeker, and now officially supports an *Annual* concerning Merton's poetry, literature, prayer life, and social concerns as well as a quarterly *Seasonal* review in existence for over thirty years. Merton collections and Merton "reading rooms "can be found in libraries, monasteries, on college campuses and certainly in private homes. Yogananda has active monastic and lay disciples today who gather at some 150 temples, centers, and meditation study groups on five continents. Yogananda's Self-Realization Fellowship has a very active press as well. Just as with Merton his writings and speeches are continuing to be mined and published posthumously.

Having stated that these two *strangers* never met, we stress that the joining of their similar ideas and the vast overlap in their approach to prayer and to God is by no means a "forced fit." Rather, it might provide a key to the lock of East-West understanding. Merton had stated unequivocally in *Mystics and Zen Masters* when discussing Emerson and Thoreau: "A hundred years ago America began to discover the Orient and its philosophical tradition... America did not have the patience to continue what was happily begun. The door had opened for an instant, closed again for a century...and now seems to be opening again...it is imperative for us to find out what is inside this fabulous edifice."[8] In the same essay he also stressed: " The horizons of the world are no longer confined to Europe and America. We have to gain new perspectives, and on this our spiritual and even our physical survival may depend."[9]

Yogananda had spent ten years of intensive formation (1910-1920) in the ashram of his guru-preceptor, Swami Sri Yukteshwar, who was immensely learned not only in the Vedic and Indian traditions but also in the Judeo-Christian scriptures and Western thought. Yukteshar's own param-guru (guru of his guru) had visited him and told him that in some future time he would steer an extraordinary disciple to him. This person was to be given the broadest and deepest spiritual training possible, and would, it was predicted, be sent to teach yogic meditation and prayer to the West. When Yukteshar received an invitation to attend the 1920 international conference on Religion in Boston or to send a representative in his stead to speak on "The Science of Religion" he recognized that this was the time for his disciple to go west.[10] The balance of Yogananda's life, some thirty-two years, was spent in the United States, where his Self-Realization Fellowship began in 1920 and grows today within many nations of the world.

In my preceding article the focus was on the sameness of concepts, and indeed of stressed areas of writing and teaching of these two Masters, particularly:

Jesus and Nicodemus

Both Merton and Yogananda extensively treated the New Testamental events of Christ's message to Nicodemus, stressing that moving forward in the spiritual life was nothing less than a "new birth." Clear to both was Jesus' charitable yet forthright handling of the Pharisee's obvious ignorance of spiritual matters (much of the Jewish religion had corrupted into a highly ritualistic and divisive entity, or rather schools of entities). Establishing ones life on a God-ward path was to entail a real and genuine renewal. What cannot be overstressed is their catholicity, which has little in common with the fundamentalist interpretation of "born again" which judges those not thus *"saved"* as somehow condemned.

Ecstatic moments

The spiritual life of both Yogananda and Merton sometimes spilled over into moments of standing outside the human body and seeing the deeper (and lasting) realities beyond the earthy existence which is our daily bread. Merton wrote of his "Fourth and Walnut" experience[11] of seeing in a crowd of persons of all types and stripes as surprisingly filled with God's light. Yogananda wrote of several of his own such deep catholic moments in which he celebrated the reality of the spirit content of our lives as being so paramount as to consider our earthly sojourn as "shadows on a screen" like a motion picture.[12]

False self and attachment vs. true self and renunciation

The Pauline concept of putting off the "old man" and being clothed with the "new man" has long been seen as key to the becoming of a follower of Christ. Baptism and a profession of faith will gain one entrance into the church of Christ (we refer here not to the sect, but to the spiritual group of those professing to "follow Christ"!). The life-long process of continuing with and following Christ requires an ever deepening commitment. The Apostle Paul wrote to the Colossians: "Therefore, if you be raised with Christ, seek the things that are above, where Christ is sitting at the right hand of God. Mind the things that are above, not the things that are upon the earth."[13] The Christian seeking this has not a momentary but rather a daily and continuous challenge.

Gandhi's unique mission to modern humankind

An important meeting ground of these two unknown-to-each-other spiritual masters was their recognition of the unique mission of Mohandas Gandhi. Just as Jesus was so obviously an avatar for *all humankind,* and was seen thus by Merton, the Christian, and Yogananda the Hindu, so was the Great Soul (Sanskrit "mahatma") of the twentieth century an avatar for *all humankind.* In fact, the stress of both authors was on Gandhi's teachings on *ahimsa* (non-violence) and *satyagraha* (holding fast to truth).[14,15] Both used the Sanskrit words in addition to the English as they described the divine impact of Gandhi. Yogananda described *Satyagraha* as taught by Jesus when he said in Matthew 5:39 "...resist not evil with evil, but whoever shall smite thee on thy right cheek, turn to him the other also." And Yogananda noted very specifically that after Gandhi's assassination the Vatican lovingly referred to Gandhi as "an apostle of *Christian* virtues."[16] In the same *post-mortem* tribute Yogananda quoted Albert Einstein's thoughtful comment also, "Generations to come, it may be, will scarce believe that such a one as this ever in flesh and blood walked upon the earth."

Merton was no less laudatory in his thoughtful book on the Mahatma, in which he underscored lessons of history and the Church teachings to support his basic premises of truth at all times (*satyagraha*) and peacefulness for all (*ahimsa*). He sees Gandhi as teaching in the same way as Pope John XXIII in his encyclical "Pacem in Terris."[17] In fact he held that such truths "...are required ... for anyone who is seriously interested in man's fate in the nuclear age."[18]

True self and detachment: Merton's life quest

Thomas Merton spent virtually his entire adult life in seeking to be clothed with the new man, indeed naming one of his major books *The New Man.*[19] Merton details detachment beautifully in many places, perhaps none better than in *New Seeds of Contemplation*[20] the chapter on detachment opens: "I wonder if there are twenty men alive in the world now that see things as they really are. That would mean that there were twenty men who were *free, who were not dominated or even influenced by any attachment* to any created thing or to their own selves or to any gift of God...."[21] Expressing disbelief that twenty are now living, he concludes "...there must be one or two. They are the ones who are holding everything together and keeping the universe from falling apart."

Finding and remaining with the true self is a hard-won battle. En route to being detached, the God-seeker will have initial and often periodic episodes of spiritual joy that seem to reward his placing high value on prayer, meditation, and living the inner life. These will invariably be followed by severe trial, "How many there must be who have smothered the first sparks of contemplation by piling wood on the fire before it was well lit... (and) they launch into ambitious projects for teaching and converting the whole world, when [what] God asks... is to be quiet and keep themselves at peace...."[22]

Here is an example where Merton, as a twentieth-century monastic, joins the small group of visionaries such as the author of *The Cloud of Unknowing*[23] and St. John of the Cross[24] as spiritual counselor for his readers. He warns the aspirant of closeness to God that this road will have its thorns and it rocks. Even the very act of prayer and the most sincere effort to approach God will be often rebuffed by God, testing the perseverance of the would be suitor.

During such episodes of the "dark night" God seems aloof, consolation absent and spiritual pain abounds. Here one recalls the words of the wondrous contemporary apostle of charity, Mother Teresa of Calcutta, describing her yearning for God but numerous feelings of emptiness and separation "The more I want him, the less I am wanted...there is that separation—that terrible emptiness—that feeling of the absence of God."[25] Merton assures us that "The Dark Night, the crisis of suffering that rends our roots out of this work, is a pure gift of God."[26] He further expounds that "...to rest in the beauty of God as a pure concept...is perhaps the highest pleasure ... [but] it must not be confused with supernatural contemplation." This perhaps sums up his own spiritual journey as Merton prayed, found both "the world" and solitude, and confronted his own fear, weakness, and strength in Christ. He concludes that "If we resolutely face our cowardice and confess it to God, no doubt He will one day take pity on us, and show us the way to freedom in detachment."[27]

Yogananda on detachment and finding the true self

For Yogananda the journey toward the New Man was also the main focus, for himself and for his students and disciples. He continually calls it the journey from:

> ...self to Self. Self is capitalized to denote the soul, man's true identity, in contradistinction to the ego or pseudo soul, the lower self with which man temporarily identifies through ignorance of his real nature. Self-realization is the knowing—in body, mind, and soul—that we are one with the omnipresence of God; those we do not have to pray that it come to us, that we are not merely near it at all times, but that God's omnipresence is our omnipresence; that we are just as much a part of Him now as we ever will be. All we have to do is improve our knowing.[28]

In the same volume he elucidates:

> The soul need acquire nothing .... The moment man's consciousness transcends body identification into Self-realization; the soul's contact with God becomes manifest, its God-essence revealed from beneath the wisdom-seared veil of ignorance.[29]

For Yogananda, Yoga and meditation (perhaps better stated *yogic-meditation*) is the route by which persons pursue the "remembering" that each of us, in our soul or real self, is a spark from the very divinity of God. By adopting the lifestyle of a yoga practitioner one moves from self to Self. Yoga is the process of reversing the flow of energy and consciousness from the lower centers of the self (whose foci are concerns with the body's functions shared with animals—viz., survival, nourishment, elimination, reproduction, power, and control) to those functions shared with higher creatures, and indeed with the Creator (love, free choice, judgment, faith, intelligence, ethics). He explains, "Yoga is a simple process of reversing the ordinary outward flow of energy and consciousness so that the mind becomes a dynamic center of direct perception—no longer dependent upon the fallible senses but capable of actually experiencing Truth."[30]

In an address entitled "The Yoga Ideal of Renunciation Is for All"[31] Yogananda asserts that "the way of complete renunciation is embraced joyously by those who want to see God, and naught else but God. He reveals Himself to those who live the renunciant's creed 'God is my life...my only Goal.'" Dealing with the obvious situation of persons who have already incurred obligations in the world, he continues:

> Yoga means "union," the path of Yoga is the science of unifying the soul with God [and]...is not restricted to the monastic in the cloister, [but extends] to the house-holder in the world. The purpose of renunciation is to pursue God... in the path of renunciation... of everything that stands in the way of one's search for God. *Yoga shows the way to inner freedom from such obstructions.*[32]

Here he meets Merton's seeking of the "one or two" who are "free... not dominated or even influenced by any attachment to any created thing." Both these enlightened masters see detachment as freedom, as being the element which "holds everything together and keep[s] the universe from falling apart."[33]

Merton and the twenty-first century

The passages analyzed above serve to illustrate remarkable congruence in these Eastern and Western God-seekers. The pairing of Yogananda with Merton shows how such Masters have little difficulty in holding in high esteem other God-seekers and their approaches to prayer, contemplation and indeed the most intimate efforts to relate to God.

This is quite different from the nineteenth and early twentieth-century needs of various western churches, sects, and hierarchical groups to use many resources for polemics, apologetics and, in fact, for "fighting" with those of a differing tradition.

Vatican II stance on East/West and freedom of religion

Some three years before Merton's journey East his own church had published two documents which removed much of the negativism of the Catholic Church-vs.-the rest of the world. In October 1965 "Nostra Aetate"[34] was promulgated by then Pope Paul VI as the official Catholic position on non-Christian religions. The document, expressing the will and teaching of the entire worldwide body of bishops of the Church, began by acknowledging the close ties being forged daily by peoples who have differing religious traditions. It pointed out that all have "... one origin, God, and one final Goal, also God. (Further)... his saving design extends to all persons whom he intends to unite in the Holy City, ablaze with the glory of God...where the nations will walk in light."[35]

Nor does the document damn any group with faint praise. Rather it notes strongly that the human condition is addressed in depth by Hindus, Buddhists, and of course Muslims and Jews, who come directly from God's working through Abraham as a common earthly father. It praises the Hindus' "flight to God with love and trust," and points out Hinduism has "searching philosophical inquiry, seek[ing] freedom from the anguish of our human condition by...ascetical practices [and] profound meditation."[36]

The Vatican document states Buddhism "...teaches a way by which men, in a devout and confident spirit, may be able either to acquire the state of perfect liberation, or attain, by ...higher help, supreme illumination."[37] In one line of expressing the inanity of bigotry, the document adds that "the Catholic Church rejects nothing that is true and holy...and she regards with sincere reverence [that]...reflect[s] a ray of that Truth which enlightens all men."[38] Muslims are also regarded "with esteem," in particular their worship of the one God, devotion to Christ as prophet and to his virgin Mother. The document praises their continuous stream of prayers to God for his goodness and as humanity's great creator and helper.

The Jewish religion is treated with high respect due to the common history of Judaism and Christianity. Both share in large measure the same bible as God's word given to us. Dealing with the ancient "Christ killer" accusation that somehow justified poor treatment of Jews by members of its own church, the Council and Paul VI says without equivocation that "some Jews" in the time of Christ worked with Romans for the crucifixion, but that "...the Jews should not be presented as rejected or accursed by God, as if this followed from Holy Scriptures." The document concludes "...no foundation...remains for any theory or practice that leads to discrimination between man and man or people and people, so far as their human dignity and the rights flowing from it are concerned."[39]

Published some seven weeks later was the Vatican document entitled Dignitas Humana, "Declaration on Religious Freedom," on December 7, 1965. In it the Council and Paul VI assert without equivocation its teaching that "...God himself has made known to mankind the way in which men are to serve Him, and thus be saved in Christ and come to blessedness...[and this is the role of] the Catholic and Apostolic Church."[40]

Equally unequivocal is its assertion that "... [all men have] immunity from coercion in civil society...This Vatican Council declares that the human person has a right to religious freedom ... [which is] a civil right."[41] Later it clarifies that "...a wrong is done when government imposes upon its people by force or fear or other means, the *profession or repudiation of any religious community.*"[42] Thus any form of official atheism by which free expression and practice of religion is forbidden or any form of theocracy whereby a religion is obligated are both always and totally unjust—a violation of basic civil rights.

Teachings of Vatican II and Merton in relation to Yogananda

In his posthumously published *magnum opus, The Second Coming of Christ: The Resurrection of the Christ Within You,*[43] Paramahansa Yogananda devotes Discourse 75, the last chapter in the two-volume work to the matter of "salvation through Christ." In this extraordinary chapter he carefully eschews the assertion that some "...rationalizing minds have proposed that when Jesus was crucified he did not actually die, but remained in a temporary state of suspended animation and later revived himself (or was taken from the tomb by his disciples and revived)...*This is not so*...Jesus completely left his body. His life and consciousness fled not only from the physical muscles and heart, but also from the spine and brain. He gave up the ghost."[44] This Hindu-educated lover of Christ clearly separates himself from those who would water down the death and resurrection of Jesus, the basis of Christian faith, firmly asserting that "he lived again in his resurrected form."[45] I quote his passage on salvation;

> Jesus emphasized in his last instruction to the Apostles their part in his ongoing *work of salvation*: "Go ye, therefore, and teach all nations, baptizing them in the name of the Father, and of the Son, and of the Holy Ghost: teaching them to observe all things whatsoever I have commanded you: and, lo, I am with you always even

unto the end of the world." And "He that *believeth and is baptized shall be saved*; but he that believeth not shall be damned." That is, any person, of any race or nationality, who *"believeth" (knows his own Self-realization) and who received the spiritual baptism of immersion in the Holy Ghost Cosmic Vibration, ("Son") and Cosmic Consciousness ("the Father") "shall be saved."* Those who cling to ignorance and thereby shut out the redeeming power condemn themselves to remain in the "hell" of the sufferings inherent in material consciousness.[46]

He concludes that "Those who observe the holy precepts of eternal truth will be in …Christ…even unto the end of the world."[47] Jesus is declaring that those disciples who maintain Christ-consciousness would have communion with him each moment—beginning in this world and continuing into the next. In fact, Jesus was to send the Spirit in order to facilitate this continuous living-in-Christ. Evident to Yogananada is that "salvation" is not merely one's future, but finding God in the Self right now.

Merton understood that the awakening to our "Inner Self" bears great similarity. Living in Christ begins when one realizes even in inchoate form that "…he is not his false self after all, and that he has all along been nothing else but his real…self, and nothing more, without glory, without self-aggrandizement, without self-righteousness, and without self-concern."[48] This very basic understanding of Merton's concept of self-realization has an interesting history.

In 1948 he had written, in response to the request of a poet-scholar at St. Mary's (Indiana) a small treatise named "What is Contemplation?" He kept a copy and mulled it over the years, and in 1959 enlarged it. Still unpublished in 1968 and having been embellished and altered for some twenty years, he gave it to Dan Walsh, an old friend. Walsh read it after Merton left for Asia, shared it with the Carmelite nuns of Kentucky, who also saw the work as a large contribution to understanding of spiritual development of the true self, and in fact the immense discovery of the role of the inner life in the development of a God-seeker of any cultural or religious background. William H. Shannon, long a contributor to propagating, editing, and publishing Merton studies, received the manuscript around 1999 and had permission from the Merton Trust to edit and publish *The Inner Experience*. Posthumously published in 2003, it will likely become a prime source in helping others find a life lived in the Spirit.

Among key insights on the topic of self-realization Merton posits that there is an infinite "...gulf between the being of God and the being of our soul, between the 'I' of the Almighty and our own inner 'I'. Yet paradoxically our inmost 'I' exists in God and God dwells in it."[49]

Merton had already noted that the God seeker of any religious or cultural or ethnic stripe will invariably see his *inner self* as "....not...like the motor of a car...It is our entire substantial reality itself, on its highest and post-personal...level...our spiritual life when it is most alive." He continues "If awakened it communicates a new life...it is not so much... (what) we have but something we are."[50]

Merton first recounts a Zen example of the awakening of the inner Self, in which it is called the "real self," which he says is "...beyond the division between self and not-self, and is a moment when mind doors burst open...to reveal (ones) 'original self' or 'suchness.'"[51] Such an instant in the life of Zen master Chao-pien is summarized in a four-line poem (as are many Chinese life lessons):

> *Devoid of thought, I sat quietly by the desk in my official room,*
> *With my fountain-mind undisturbed, as serene as water;*
> *A sudden crash of thunder, the mind doors burst open,*
> *And lo, there sits the old man in all his homeliness.*[52]

Merton comments that his "mind undisturbed" is like the Christian who meditates in the "cloud of unknowing." It is also reminiscent of John of the Cross as he began his *Ascent to Mount Carmel*, "My house being stilled."[53] Like Chio-pen, St. John experienced "...a self-realization in which the false, exterior self is caught in all its naked nothingness and immediately dispelled as an illusion."[54] In other words, the lesser reality of our self gives way to the greater Self in us.

Continuing to describe a Christian approach to the awakening of the inner self, he asserts that while "In Zen there seems to be no effort to get *beyond* the inner self.... [i]n Christianity the inner self is simply a stepping stone to an awareness of God. Man is the image of God, and his inner self is a kind of mirror in which God not only sees Himself, but reveals Himself to the 'mirror' in which He is reflected."[55] At this point faith must enter. Such faith is a pure gift of God by which he begins to awaken the soul to show the vast difference between God seen in the mirror and seen "face-to-face." This latter is the life-long mission of the contemplative, and indeed many (most?) Christians who begin this journey may well not finish it in this lifetime.

Merton also examines the Rhenish Dominican mystic, John Tauler, for whom the inner self is the "ground" or "center" of the soul:

> Now man...enters into the temple (his inner self) in which...he finds God dwelling and at work...like something that springs up from the ground of the soul...as from a fountain... [for] a fountain is better than a cistern.[56]

On another occasion, Tauler said that upon thus "seeing" the Godhead, one "...look(s) upon him with great and humble fear and denial of oneself....The Lord then comes like a flash of lightning; he fills the ground of the soul with light and wills to establish Himself there as the Master Workman. As soon as one is conscious of the presence of the Master, one must, in all passivity, abandon the work to Him."[57] This "denial of oneself" is the personal *epiphany moment* which enables one to see the false separation of self from Self.

At this point in his analysis Merton again repairs to one of his faithful mentors, John of the Cross, who assures him that after "finding God," followed by submission and by darkness and spiritual yearning that seems quite unrewarded, this journey of discovery "...brings us into the depths of our own being and releases us that we may voyage beyond ourselves to God... [and be] "transformed in God...Who dwells in us...."[58] Merton then describes the true contemplative as "...the one best attuned to the logos of man's...situation, immersed in its mystery...in harmony with the Tao."[59] Students of Merton are more and more seeing the posthumous (2003) editing of *The Inner Experience* by Shannon as having given them his later and perhaps more mature thought on the radical *sameness* of all *true* religion in leading one to his/her full identity with God.

Self-realization in Yogananda's writings

Yogananda had received a specific commission from his guru, Swami Sri Yukteshar of Puri, India to write a spiritual commentary on the *Bagavad Gita*, the greatest scripture in Hinduism. The *Gita* recounts how Lord

Krishna guided his disciple, Arjuna, to victory at the battle of Kurukshetra. He fulfilled the commission by writing *The Bagavad Gita: Royal Science of God-Realization*.[60] Posthumously edited and printed in two volumes, the book expounds the process of "realizing the Self," which is going from the self (the pseudo soul, or external body and action) to the Self (the discovery of God within). The *Gita* has often been explained wrongly as describing a military or conventional war, but a proper reading shows that it is the battle of everyone in moving from the dependence on the physical needs to union with God.

The process begins by searching to be free from physical dependency, beginning with the coccygeal chakra: "Yoga refers to this power flowing from the coccyx to Spirit as the awakened kundalini."[61] After years (and indeed Yogananda considers over various lifetimes of incarnations) of yogic meditation, the yogi will learn to withdraw his life force from the senses and focus it in the single eye (the point between the eyebrows). He then will find himself in a joyful state of breathlessness in which "He thrills to see streams of prana rolling backward from the countless cells and ascending the spinal tunnel through the coiled stairway (kundalini), out from the single-eye passage in the forehead into a subtle astral body."[62] He clarifies the process by explaining that the coiled creative force at the base of the astral spine, the kundalini, has always been symbolized as a serpent. When this creative force is "asleep" in delusion, it flows down and outward and feeds all the senses, uncontrolled, its stinging venom causes insatiable lusts. "But when the pure kundalini force is 'awakened' by the yogi, it rises to the brain and is transformed into the bliss of Spirit. This uplifting serpentine current is *vasuki*, the supreme force for human liberation."[63]

Yogananda perceives the purpose of our time on earth is to ascend the six spinal centers, reinforcing the human consciousness progressively with greater and greater lights, until one is able to unite with the all pervading, thousand-rayed brilliance in the highest center in the brain. This *ascent of consciousness* through the spine may be achieved slowly through right actions and right thoughts. The yogi, however, chooses the quicker and more scientific method of meditation.

Yogananda perceives that the internal consciousness of ordinary people operates only from the lumbar, sacral, and coccygeal centers that direct all material sensory perceptions and enjoyments. However "The divine lovers and celestial poets work from the heart center. The calm unshaken yogi operates from the cervical center. He who can feel his presence in the entire vibratory creation has awakened the medullary and Christ centers. The illumined yogi functions in the cerebral center of Cosmic Consciousness; he may be spoken of as an ascended yogi."[64] Thus Yogananda summarizes his mission as teaching humanity, Eastern and Western, to be free of all physical and karmic restraints in one lifetime.

A succinct (113 pages) volume of Yogananda's basic teaching on Jesus has been recently published entitled *The Yoga of Jesus*.[65] This well edited and annotated volume focuses on the basics of Jesus' teaching during his three-year ministry. The principal focus is on "the Kingdom of God within you."[66] Yogananda begins with the encounter of Jesus with the Pharisees. "And when he was demanded of the Pharisees, when the kingdom of God should come, he answered and said, 'the kingdom of God' cometh not with observation: Neither shall they say, 'Lo here!' or 'lo there!' for, behold, the kingdom of God is within you."[67]

Jesus had long made the finding of the kingdom of God as the centerpiece of his mission (examples are such as: "seek ye first the kingdom of God and his justice," the prayer "thy kingdom come," "unless a man be born of water and of the Spirit, he cannot enter into the kingdom of God"). Further he taught "if thy eye offends thee, pluck it out: it is better for thee to enter into the kingdom of God with one eye, than having two eyes be cast into hell fire." And "I am the way, the truth, and the life: no man cometh unto the Father but by me." Clearly union with God and belonging to his "kingdom" were not from "observation," that is, visible to sight and audible—but humanity must find God within. Yogananda is stressing that the kingdom of God is not separate from the kingdom of matter, but exists both within it—pervading it in subtle form as its origin and sustainer—and beyond it, exists in the infinite mansions of the Father beyond the circumscribed physical cosmos."[68] Every person can find God waiting within by delving in meditation, transcending human consciousness and reaching the higher states of Christ Consciousness and cosmic consciousness. By yogic meditation (specifically the ancient method of Kriya yoga) humankind can withdraw the mind from material objects (of the external senses) and enter the blissful visions of the realms of eternal light. So liberation begins in this life and continues after the body breathes its last breath.

Yogananda indicates the "steps" to bliss are the same as those taught by Patanjali:[69] 1. Yama (abstaining from injury to others, falsehood, stealing, incontinence, and covetousness); 2. Niyama (purity of body and mind, self study and devotion); 3. Asana (disciplining the body to stillness and erectness in meditation); 4. Pranayama (life-force control that calms the heart and breath, removing sensory distractions); 5. Pratyahara (interiorization and mental stillness, resulting from withdrawal of the mind from the senses); 6. Dhyana (one-pointed concentration on God—cosmic consciousness); and 7. Samadhi (union with God the realization of the soul's oneness with God). These details are provided to illustrate that the Hindu perspective, as well as the Buddhist perspective better known to Merton, might have been fodder for his further work had he lived longer to guide us eastward.

Awakenings: Thomas Merton's final communications

About midway into his 1968 journey Merton sent a "circular letter" to the hundreds of his then current correspondents. He sent it to Brother Patrick (as his secretary) who would then copy and send it out in mimeograph form. In this November 1968 circular letter he spoke gratefully of his eight days of retreat and prayer in Dharamsala, where he had the three long visits with the Dalai Lama. He described him as fair, candid, curious about Christian monasticism, a leader and a scholar "...who has obviously received a remarkable monastic formation."[70] Merton found that Tibetan Buddhists have a lot of scientific knowledge of "the mind" and experiment with meditation to discover ways to improve their mindfulness and living in the moment.

Merton pointed out as well that Tibetan Buddhists also spoke of higher forms of prayer, finding that their meditations were simple, but based on a spiritual life which they held *must* be of "total dedication, continued effort, experienced guidance, real discipline, and the combination of wisdom and method."[71] Merton was quite impressed with the level of mysticism of the Dalai Lama and that of many monks in his monastery.

Merton also reported of his learning about Sufism (Muslim) and other forms of Buddhism, concluding that the East has many experts in meditation to benefit Christians and others, and concluded "I also hope

I can bring back to my monastery something of the Asian wisdom with which I am fortunate to be in contact."[72]

Implications

Any "conclusion" I may make within a speculative survey is tinged by admitting a personal history composed of a highly formalistic background in Catholic Theology and Sacred Scripture (Roman Catholic seminary 1954-1961 and serving as active priest over nine years before resigning from that commitment). Clearly one should posit a similar Roman Catholic training for Merton, given his eight years of formation leading to his priestly ordination, followed by nineteen years of being a choir monk. He differed greatly, however, from the "average monk" both because of his status in the world as a talented author on spiritual matters with correspondence from hundreds of fellow God-seekers of all hues and stripes, both religious and ethnic, and also because of his growing prayer life.

The involvement with persons from such diversity may be seen as an obvious advantage, yet to many it was an uncomfortable departure from the strict doctrinal separatism. Thanks to the papacy of John XXIII ecumenism was being encouraged, yet nonetheless many fellow Catholics of the 1950s and 1960s viewed such sharing with "non-Christians" as somehow dangerous.

Merton explained how he felt quite clearly, "...we have reached a stage of (long-overdue) religious maturity at which it may be possible for someone to remain perfectly faithful to a Christian and Western monastic commitment, and yet to learn in depth from, say, a Buddhist or Hindu discipline and experience. I believe that some of us need to do this ...to improve the quality of our own monastic life."[73] Merton contends that prayerful investigation and interchange with those of different faith formations is enriching to both groups, and is fully within the gospel of Christ and the history of the Christian community. Jesus was a middle-Easterner and Merton had a deep awareness of that. For me I see a clear advantage both to the Christian and to his spiritual belief today in becoming aware of parallels such as have been pointed out in this article.

I suggest that reading Thomas Merton and Paramahansa Yogananda with a mind that is both prayerful and analytic should lead one to conclude that their understanding of the New Testamental teachings is intimately the same. This sameness can be documented on such matters as the divinity of Christ, the reality of his death and resurrection, Jesus' commission to the apostles.

In studying these two religious sages it is equally obvious that Merton and Yogananda (who never met) had large agreement that we delude ourselves into over-identifying with the material life, and that the intimate unity of God with humankind is much deeper, and that the Divine energy and essence is immediately available to those who prepare to receive it.

Merton and Yogananda agreed that the bliss of heaven is more available to us than the air we breathe, and that we can make large strides toward that realization. Both teach continuously that the only obstacle is our own ignorance and that we can rise from our slumber to the reality of our being heirs and children of God, whose birthright includes our Father/Mother's wisdom and understanding.

Perhaps the most remarkable advantage to such East-West dialogue and shared prayer is to persons interested in deepening their relationship to God. Merton was quite at home in discussing meditation with the Dahli Lama and in praying with him and his monks. For both of these seekers the understanding and deepening of the concept of the self and the Self was real.

Merton and Yogananda both experienced that upon "awakening" to the omnipresent Christ-consciousness one's life changes "right now," not in some distant future. The most secure conclusion to this student, therefore, is that the time is now for deepening the East-West dialogue.

Notes

1. Merton, Thomas, *The Asian Journal of Thomas Merton,* eds. Naomi Burton Stone, Br. Patrick Hart & James Laughlin (New York: New Directions, 1973), pp. 4-5.
2. Merton, Thomas, *The Intimate Merton: His Life from His Journals*, eds. Patrick Hart and Jonathan Montaldo (San Francisco: Harper, 1999), pp. 221-22.
3. Merton, *The Asian Journal of Thomas Merton*, pp. 344-47.
4. Merton, *The Asian Journal of Thomas Merton*, pp. 31-33, *et seq.*
5. Griffiths, Bede, *Return to the Center* (Springfield, Il: Temple Gate Publishing, 1976).
6. Farge, Emile, "Thomas Merton and Paramahansa Yogananda: Two Prayerful Mergings ofCult and Culture," *The Merton Annual,* Volume 20 (Louisville: Fons Vitae, 2007), pp. 164-84.
7. Farge, *The Merton Annual*, p. 165.

8. Merton, Thomas, *Mystics and Zen Masters* (New York: Farrar, Straus & J Giroux, 1967), p. 69.
9. Merton, *Mystics and Zen Masters*, p. 80.
10. Yogananda, Paramahansa, *Autobiography of a Yogi* (Los Angeles: Self-Realization Press), 1946, p. 242 et seq.
11. Merton, Thomas, *Conjectures of a Guilty Bystander,* (Garden City, NY: Doubleday, 1966), pp. 140-41.
12. Yogananda, *Autobiography of a Yogi*, pp. 142-43.
13. Epistle to Colossians, 3, 1-3.
14. Merton, Thomas, *Gandhi on Non-Violence* (New York: New Directions) 1965, p. 4.
15. Yogananda, *Autobiography of a Yogi*, pp. 419-37.
16. Yogananda, *Autobiography of a Yogi*, pp. 436-37.
17. Merton, *Gandhi on Non-Violence*, pp. 13-14.
18. Merton, *Gandhi on Non-Violence*, p. 20.
19. Merton, Thomas, *The New Man* (New York: Farrar, Straus & Cudahy, 1961).
20. Merton, Thomas, *New Seeds of Contemplation,* (New York: New Directions, 1961).
21. Merton, *New Seeds of Contemplation*, p. 203.
22. Merton, *New Seeds of Contemplation*, p. 210.
23. Johnson, William, (ed.), *The Cloud of Unknowing.*
24. *The Collected Works of Saint John of the Cross*, trans. K. Kavanaugh and O. Rodriguez (Washington, DC: ICS Publications, 1991), pp. 461 et seq.
25. Kolodiejchuk, Brian, *Mother Teresa Come Be My Light* (New York: Doubleday Publishing, 2007), p. 164.
26. Merton, *New Seeds of Contemplation*, p. 213.
27. Merton, *New Seeds of Contemplation*, p. 216.
28. Yogananda, Paramahansa, *The Second Coming of Christ* (Los Angeles: Self-Realization Fellowship Press, 2004), pp. xxi-xxii.
29. Yogananda, *The Second Coming of Christ*, pp. 322-23.
30. Yogananda, Paramahansa, *The Yoga of Jesus* (Los Angeles: Self-Realization Fellowship Press, 2007), p. ix.
31. Yogananda, Paramahansa, *The Divine Romance,* (Los Angeles: Self-Realization Fellowship Press, 2000), pp. 230-41.
32. Yogananda, *The Divine Romance*, pp. 233-34.
33. Merton, *New Seeds of Contemplation*, p. 206.
34. Pope Paul VI, "*Nostra Aetate,*" Vatican City Document, 1965.
35. *Nostra Aetate*, p. 1.
36. *Nostra Aetate*, p. 1.
37. *Nostra Aetate*, p. 1.
38. *Nostra Aetate*, p. 1.
39. *Nostra Aetate*, p. 2.
40. Pope Paul VI, "*Dignitas Humanae,*" Vatican City Document, 1965, p. 1.
41. *Dignitas Humanae*, p. 2.
42. *Dignitas Humanae*, p. 7.
43. Yogananda, *The Second Coming of Christ*, pp. 1493-524.

44. Yogananda, *The Second Coming of Christ*, p. 1506.
45. Yogananda, *The Second Coming of Christ*, p. 1508
46. Yogananda, *The Second Coming of Christ*, p. 1520.
47. Yogananda, *The Second Coming of Christ*, p. 1520.
48. Merton, Thomas, *The Inner Experience*, ed. William H. Shannon (San Francisco: HarperCollins, 2003), p. 11.
49. Merton, *The Inner Experience*, p. 12.
50. Merton, *The Inner Experience*, p. 6.
51. Merton, *The Inner Experience*, p. 8.
52. Merton, *The Inner Experience*, p. 9.
53. *The Collected Works of Saint John of the Cross*, p. 113.
54. Merton, *The Inner Experience*, p. 10.
55. Merton, *The Inner Experience*, p. 11.
56. Merton, *The Inner Experience*, pp. 14-15 (here Merton quotes from a sermon of Taulor).
57. Merton, *The Inner Experience*, p. 14.
58. Merton, *The Inner Experience*, p. 17.
59. Merton, *The Inner Experience*, p. 11.
60. Yogananda, Paramahansa, *The Bagavad Gita: Royal Science of God Realization* (Los Angeles, Self-Realization Press, 1995).
61. Yogananda, *The Bagavad Gita: Royal Science of God-Realization*, p. 18.
62. Yogananda, *The Bagavad Gita: Royal Science of God-Realization*, p. 727.
63. Yogananda, *The Bagavad Gita: Royal Science of God-Realization,* p. 793.
64. Yogananda, *The Bagavad Gita: Royal Science of God-Realization*, p. 797.
65. Yogananda, Paramahansa, *The Yoga of Jesus: Understanding the Hidden Teachings of the Gospels* (Los Angeles: Self-Realization Press, 2007).
66. Yogananda, *The Yoga of Jesus*, pp. 100-13.
67. Luke 17, 20-21.
68. Yogananda, *The Yoga of Jesus*, p. 103.
69. Yogananda, *The Yoga of Jesus*, p. 105.
70. Merton, *The Asian Journal of Thomas Merton*, p. 322.
71. Merton, *The Asian Journal of Thomas Merton*, p. 322.
72. Merton, *The Asian Journal of Thomas Merton*, p. 325.
73. Merton, *The Asian Journal of Thomas Merton*, p. 313.

"FINE AND DANGEROUS"
Teaching Merton

David A. King

Introduction

In the summer of 2008, while teaching a course on the literature and films associated with the Vietnam War, I tried to give my students a sense of the context of 1968, the year in which the Tet Offensive dramatically altered the American public's perception of that tragic conflict. I told my students that 1968 was arguably one of the most tumultuous years in American history. My students agreed with me, and nodded solemnly as I recited the events associated with that pivotal year. They all knew, of course, about the shocking assassinations of Martin Luther King, Jr. and Robert Kennedy. They knew about the riots at the Democratic National Convention in Chicago. They knew about the Beatles' trip to India, and other events associated with the popular culture and music of the era. A few even knew about the student uprisings in Paris. Then, almost as an afterthought, I said, "Oh, and Thomas Merton died accidentally following a talk at a conference in Bangkok, Thailand." In this class of thirty bright, curious, young American college students, not one knew about Thomas Merton. In fact, no one had even heard of him.

These students' ignorance about Merton should have surprised me. In the forty years since his death, Merton's reputation as a gifted monk and artist has continued to grow. His work has never been more available, and the wealth of excellent scholarship associated with his writing has continued to attract the attention of a secular audience. In its growing desire for contemplation, peace, and solitude this new audience, in fact, represents perhaps Merton's ideal reader. We live in an age marked by obsession with the present moment, a madness for speed, and a rampant consumerism, and Merton's work offers of course an antidote for these skewed values. Yet today, most college students—and indeed, many academics—remain unfamiliar with Merton's life and writing. This article argues that we should learn about Merton.

American college courses in the humanities have always considered the American contemplative tradition; Emerson and Thoreau have been part of the American canon for generations. It is surprising then, that in an age so obviously in need of contemplation, Merton remains for many teachers a kind of enigma. That he was a Christian, a convert to Catholicism, and a cloistered Cistercian monk obviously makes Merton suspicious to many in the academy. This essay insists that Merton can be taught and appreciated in a public, secular setting. Indeed, this article asserts that Merton may in fact be best understood in such a context.

I propose to argue that Merton can and should be taught as other American contemplatives are taught; that he can and should be considered as one of the best writers to come out of the post-war Beat Generation; and that he can and should be understood as one of the most provocative voices of the Cold-War period and the 1960s. Furthermore, aside from these secular contexts, I also believe that a discussion of monasticism and the contemplative life can give today's students—and teachers—an understanding of vocation and a greater sense of what a college education should mean.

Merton always saw himself as living a life of paradox, and ultimately that is perhaps what students find most attractive about him. A rebel by nature, he took a vow of obedience. A cloistered, silent monk and later a hermit, he nonetheless spoke loudly to the world. A religious bound to one of the oldest and strictest orders, he intuitively understood—years before they became mainstream—new experimental forms of writing. And long before global learning and ecumenism became popular, Merton was looking to the East and other religious traditions.

A good teacher can convey all of this to students, but the best teachers can also show that Merton's religion and spirituality, and above all his emphasis on authenticity and love, are of crucial relevance to people now.

In addition, this article offers practical advice on teaching Merton in a variety of contexts and mentions some of the most helpful resources for introducing this great American writer and thinker to a new, young audience.

An argument for Merton's inclusion in the academy
Walk into any college lecture hall in the United States today, and you will find yourself practically buzzing along with the wireless current that throbs in the room. The American campus blinks, beeps, vibrates, and hums in an electronic cacophony of cell phones, I-Pods, pagers, laptops, Blackberries, Palm Pilots, and other devices that in the name of communication have isolated students from their faculty, and from one another, farther than ever before. In the midst of this environment, the human voice strains to be heard, while the printed word, the book, seems almost a quaint relic from another age. If the source of information does not glow, or come with headphones, it often seems most students do not want to know about it. Faculty office hours have become obsolete, as few students ever visit in person, but a few professors in my department still keep them. Sitting in the dim light of their offices, the door ajar in anticipation, they look almost in need of dusting. Even the telephone conversation seems antiquated. Instead, the contact most students seek from their professors is electronic. Urgent emails, often anonymous and full of misspellings and grammatical errors, demand instant attention to matters concerning due dates and grades. If all this sounds like grousing, I suppose it is. Although I am still a fairly young professor myself, I often yearn for the days when faculty and students actually *spoke* to one another.

In a familiar and often quoted passage from Merton's *The Seven Storey Mountain*, the new monk and young writer, brimming with idealism, remembers his own college days at Columbia, and recalls that for him "October is a fine and dangerous season in America....you go to college, and every course in the catalog looks wonderful. The names of the subjects all seem to lay open the way to a new world."[1] For many public college students now, college is hardly an adventure. It is instead their logical, required, practical duty as pragmatic and motivated members of our society. Some view their education as a chore, their classes as yet another weekly task to be completed after they clock out of their mundane jobs, positions that occupy far more of their time and thought than the coursework they pursue. Often, they seem to plod from course to course—uninspired, disengaged, and unsympathetic to new ideas. They seem to have come to college on a whim, and are likely to view college as an accelerated 13th grade, in which they will be coddled, and guided, and tolerated, just as they always have been. They are bemused. They are entitled. They are also, perhaps, a little scared. Many of them retain Merton's own early "[suspicion] of literature, poetry—the things towards which [his] nature drew [him]—on the grounds that they might lead to a sort of futile estheticism, a philosophy of 'escape.'"[2]

But in the back of their minds, these students sense—indeed, I believe they *know*—that college is supposed to be different. They are simply waiting for someone to show them how. Upon their matriculation, these contemporary college students open themselves to the very real possibility that their lives will be touched, and changed, by mystery and wonder. As a student at Columbia, you may recall, Merton himself almost walked out one of the most exciting experiences of his entire education. Realizing that he had entered the wrong room, "that [Professor Mark Van Doren's class] was not the class I was supposed to be taking,"

> I got up to go out. But when I got to the door I turned again and went back and sat down where I had been, and stayed there...It was the best course I ever had at college. And it did me the most good, in many different ways. It was the only place where I ever heard anything really sensible said about any of the things that were really fundamental—life, death, time, love, sorrow, fear, wisdom, suffering, eternity.[3]

Merton had a revelation in Van Doren's class, and ultimately that is what I what I hope for my own students who read Merton's work. The study of any classic text, and especially the study of a religious writer's work, should in the end result in an epiphany. My students arrive at such affirming realizations all the time.

One semester, after reading just *The Seven Storey Mountain*, one student wrote "Thomas Merton understands that so many young people in

America fail because they don't realize that a successful future is meaningless without God."[4] Another said, "Just recently, I was having a hard time, and I thought to myself 'How would Merton handle it?' I can honestly say [The Seven Storey Mountain] has changed my life...it's almost like a second Bible to me." Still another wrote that "Our world today is afraid, just like Merton's generation was afraid. That was what I really took from [his work], that people of all times have fear, whether it's of atomic bombs or pipe bombs. But Merton teaches us that we don't have to be afraid if we have faith."

These comments represent wisdom, maturity, and understanding. Are not these the aims of all education? Merton knew that all monks sensed the futility of a life based on materialism; in *The Waters of Siloe* he writes that "there is something in their hearts that tells them they cannot be happy in an atmosphere where people are looking for nothing but their own pleasure and advantage and comfort and success."[5] It is not as eloquent as Merton's prose, but when an eighteen-year-old boy tells me "Merton has shown me that it's not the size of your bank account that matters, but the size of your soul," hasn't he arrived at the same important conclusion? I will share two other comments from student essays that express how students learn from Merton what I hope they will learn. One young man writes that "Merton reminds me that all of us have a void, or emptiness, that needs filling. Most of us, myself included, try to fill that void with the things of the world. [*The Seven Storey Mountain*] was difficult for me to read, and I found some of it boring, but it has a universal message of hope that all college students need to know." Finally, another student writes "For me, the best part of the book was that Merton teaches that silence, or quiet time, is often more important than all the demands and responsibilities of life that do not really matter in the long run."

Comments such as these thrill me as a teacher, and they would I believe thrill Merton too, who once wrote to a group of Smith College students who had read his books that "for a writer there is surely not much that can be more rewarding than the fact of being really read and understood and appreciated."[6] Do all of my students arrive at this sort of insight? Of course not. I still suffer comments resembling these: "There is too much Latin in this book, why I'll never know"; "It's obvious through this boring book that Merton was an intelligent man";

"I feel that Merton was more of a writer than a monk"; and "There was so much information in this book, my mind and body physically ached," but the majority of my students experience, often for the first time, the impact a great book can have on one's own life.[7] The professor who dares to teach Thomas Merton in the contemporary American university also opens herself to the possibility of an epiphany. She may find, as I have discovered, that teaching Merton opens a place for silence in the midst of chaos, restores the value of contemplation even in an atmosphere of pragmatism, and affirms the deep human need for belief. Achieving all of this, however, is not easy.

That teaching Merton is, indeed, not easy should come perhaps as a surprise for academics—particularly professors of English—for he belongs in a very real sense to a long contemplative tradition in American literature that includes writers as varied as Emerson, Thoreau, and Black Elk and encompasses as well a broad range of religious writers in English from Jonathan Edwards in America to John Henry Newman, Gerard Manley Hopkins, and C. S. Lewis in Britain. Peruse any academic anthology of British or American literature published prior to 1985, and they are all there, these writers who stressed the divine and who, in doing so, often crossed over into the secular realm. One great irony of the destruction of the conventional literary canon is that in abandoning the old stalwarts steeped in the Christian tradition, the revised approach to the college teaching of literature opened the way for voices as deeply committed to contemplation, reflection, and spirituality as Merton. This is particularly true in Native American literature. For anyone who has not looked at a college American literature anthology lately, consider the new voices that began to surface in the 1990s. More importantly consider what the voices are saying: Wovoka's "The Messiah Letter," the Navajo "Night Chant to the Sacred Mountains," The Arapaho Ghost Dance song that pleads, "Father, have pity on me." Students may no longer consider the New England Psalter, but they are likely to have read the Iroquois version of the Creation. Where their parents might have begun a study of American literature with Winthrop, Taylor, and Mather, students today may very likely begin with a reading of the Cherokee memorials for the dead.[8] I need hardly argue here, nor issue a reminder, that one version of American literature was steeped from the beginning in Christian roots, and another was embedded in a profound belief in a communion with an essentially spiritual world. The point is that in trying to lessen the value of a literature that was providential at its core, the revisionists have further exhibited the centrality of spiritual belief in this country's literature. There is a tradition and a pattern of faith in American literature, oblivious to gender or culture, which stretches from Columbus all the way to Denise Levertov, Kathy Song, and Li-Young Lee, and in spite of the secular humanists in departments of English, the spiritual voice in American letters cannot be silenced. Merton's voice needs to be heard in this chorus too.

Let me be honest: there is a litany of arguments, many of them absurd, which have kept Merton from canonical status, even as many lesser writers have been ushered into the ever bulging anthologies. Consider the comments I have heard from the very few colleagues who have read Merton: Merton's work is too personal, too self-reflective. He wrote too much. He did not write enough. He never wrote a novel (and, in fact, he wrote four). His poetry is too easy. He was subject to *censors*. *Catholic* censors. Catholic *monastic* censors. Essentially, the problem relates to context. What does one do with a monk—even a monk who was passionately committed to peace and social justice? And the doubts about monasticism essentially represent an uncertainty about God.

Of course, arguments founded upon ignorance about the inclusion of Merton in a college reading list are easily dismissed. The ones that relate to a problem with context can be answered by providing a summary of contexts in which Merton's work could be taught. The contemplative tradition aside, Merton easily fits in a discussion about the Beat Generation writers of the 1950s and early 1960s. In fact, an argument can be made that even in the late 1930s and early 1940s Merton anticipated and preceded many of the Beats' subject material and thematic concerns.[9] This is evident in the book reviews, in the unpublished manuscripts, and in the journals, particularly Volume I of the Journals, *Run to the Mountain*, in which as early as 1939 Merton was sitting in his Perry Street apartment musing on the essential divinity of poetry. By the end of the Second World War, Merton was in the monastery, but he had already considered in his unpublished drafts many of the same concerns of those young novelists—Mailer, Salinger, Knowles, Malamud, Bellow, Styron—who came of age after the war. Certainly *The Seven Storey Mountain*, which dates from this period, was not only a "religious" publishing phenomenon but also a book that addressed in coherent and convincing literary style many of the same ideas and anxieties expressed by the post-war novelists.

But Merton slips through the cracks. Even in Catholic circles, he is often not mentioned at all when people often remember Edwin O'Connor's fine novels, especially *The Edge of Sadness*. He does not fit in with John R. Powers' often funny and perceptive memoirs of American Catholic childhood prior to Vatican II. And while Graham Greene and Evelyn Waugh both translate easily and subtly to the cinema, Merton's voice is difficult, and perhaps impossible, to adapt to the screen. Walker Percy and Flannery O'Connor will always have a place in courses in Southern literature, but Merton, lacking a regional center, is overshadowed by them even though while living in Kentucky he grappled with the same racial concerns.

At times, one marvels at Merton's fear that he would become so popular that he become like a saint for children in parochial schools. However, his fear that he would be isolated, constrained into the often vacuous subgenre of "religious writing," appears to have come true. Merton's largest audience comes from informed Catholic readers, and the emphasis remains upon Catholic. Readers searching for a more obscure Merton title in their local bookstore are advised to head straight for their local Catholic bookshop; Merton is not found on the shelves of the "family" or "Christian" bookstores, and in the large chains, he is usually represented only by the early books that made him famous when he was alive. Sometimes, tucked in alphabetically between C.S. Lewis and Henri Nouwen, Merton looks rather small.

The appeal Merton holds for today's college students
Assigned to a fairly narrow range of readers, then, a paradox that would have delighted him begins to emerge: ultimately, the academy may be the *best* place in which to teach Merton, for here he is truly open to the world, and not subject solely to a religious audience's subjectivity or carefully structured parameters. That is not to say that the religious context should be avoided or ignored when teaching Merton in a secular setting; indeed, I encourage *emphasizing* the Catholic and monastic aspects of Merton's work. Students entering college in the post-9/11

world are seeking something in which to believe. Unlike their parents' generation that questioned belief, or their grandparents' generation that often had beliefs prescribed for them, these students are enthusiastic about expressing the faith they already possess, or are eager to discover a new faith. Last year, for example, when the Dalai Lama visited Atlanta, I was amazed at the number of my students—most of them Southern Baptist or from other mainline Protestant denominations—who made pilgrimages to see his public appearances and lectures. To a person, almost every student acknowledged that while they might not adhere to the Dalai Lama's religion, they respected the fact that, as they put it, *he stood for something.* I suspect that in some ways, too, the students were drawn to the media frenzy that surrounded his visit, but I also know that this generation of college students exhibits far more interest in social justice and social action than my own, and I know that many of them also have a fascination with ecumenical spirituality, particularly of the Eastern variety. When I first taught Merton in a college class fifteen years ago, I was approached by a small group of concerned students who, upon learning that I was a Catholic, earnestly inquired if I was "saved." Now, however, my students seem much more open to religions outside their own experience. In fact, it often seems that the more exotic one's faith is perceived to be, students seem more likely to be interested in it. And few things seem as exotic as monasticism.

Indeed, monastic life—a life peculiar and unknown to most young Americans—is perhaps one of the greatest attractions for collegiate readers, once they move beyond a few prejudices. Of course, here in the South, even though my campus is only about an hour's drive from the Cistercian Monastery of the Holy Spirit, a daughter-house of Gethsemani, many of my students do still harbor some suspicion about monks and monasteries. They are like Flannery O'Connor's Ms. Flood, who in disdaining the asceticism of Hazel Motes, says of him, "He might as well be one of them monks...he might as well be in a monkery."[10] Some of my students express as well Mrs. Flood's indignation that "it's not normal. It's like one of them gory stories, it's something that people have quit doing—like boiling in oil or being a saint or walling up cats. There's no reason for it. People have quit doing it."[11] Why, my students want to know, would anybody ever want to retreat into the cloister, live a life of silence and celibacy, and hide from the world? To agitate them, I sometimes answer, given the state of the world, why *wouldn't* anybody want to? To be honest, some of my students will never understand the appeal of monasticism, nor will they ever fully embrace the valuable lessons it has for the world. Although my students are curious, and more open to ecumenism than ever before, they are still the products of a noisy, hectic, and consumer society. When I take them on field trips to the Monastery of the Holy Spirit, the quiet and reflective day unravels for most of them as a shopping spree in the gift shop, where they buy as much fudge and fruitcake as they can carry.

And yet I believe for my students as Merton believed for the country: "America is discovering the contemplative life."[12] This may be especially true for our college students. If, as Merton says in *The Seven Storey Mountain*, "the monastery is a school,"[13] might I also suggest the converse, that the school should be like a monastery? Monastic life embraces community, encourages civility, and celebrates love. I hear all the time on my campus that we are part of a community, and I usually heed this assertion with distrust, but I do believe that the study of monasticism may very well add to the sense of community among twenty undergraduates. I listen to complaints from colleagues all the time, and I sometimes utter them myself, that students are disruptive, unruly, disengaged, but I am sure that sixteen weeks spent in the company of St. Benedict's ideal do much good in terms of students' emotional and intellectual maturity. I am often met with scoffs and smirking when I suggest that a good college course ought to incorporate the spirit of love—of learning, of teaching, even of one's fellows—but I fail to see how people studying a text based on love cannot also begin to feel some of that love themselves. Yet even if we do not accept spiritual parallels between a monastery and a public university, surely we can see the practical aspects the two have in common. Merton's description of Trappist monasteries in *The Waters of Siloe* as "places full of peace and contentment and joy"[14] represents precisely the ideal atmosphere students should find on a college campus. The life of a monk, I tell my students, is in many ways not unlike your own experience as a college student. Like a new monk, you too are a novice. You face new challenges, new hardships, and paradoxically, new freedoms. Merton, I tell them after we have finished reading *The Seven Storey Mountain* and are preparing for our trip to the monastery, disdained "the artificial public image which [the book] created."[15] Monks, contrary to what many of my students believe after reading *The Seven Storey Mountain*, are not perfect nor do they always seek to attain perfection. In fact, I assure my students, monks suffer the same temptations, and are susceptible to many of the same trivial concerns, that you are. I sometimes use Merton's satirical poem "A Practical Program for Monks" in class to illustrate the comparison. Although Merton and his brother monks were on a spiritual journey of profound complexity, they still had to be concerned with "mind[ing] both the clock and the Abbot."[16] The monastery, like the university, had to worry over the often unpleasant business of being a business—"in Kentucky there is also room for a little cheese."[17] And each monk, though he had a lofty spiritual purpose, might want to bend the rules just a little, for "I believe it is easier when they have ice water and even a lemon!"[18] All of this is obvious to the seasoned reader of Merton, and it is apparent to anyone who has studied monasticism. But for my students it is a revelation. When we visit the monastery, and the students have an audience with one of the more gregarious monks, they are delighted that he appears wearing a jean jacket and sock cap over his habit, smells of cigarette smoke, and expounds on the joys of listening to Bob Dylan.

Indeed, after meeting this monk, the students return to campus with renewed interest in Merton's later and more mature work because they sense that Fr. Louis might have also retained his rebellious streak even in the monastery. They are pleased to hear, on a superficial level, that he was dismayed by the cheese business and did not hesitate to say so, but more importantly, they become fascinated when they read Merton's compelling essays and letters on pacifism, nuclear disarmament, and social and racial justice. This is the Merton who speaks to youth's universal distrust of authority. This is the Merton, too, who understands youth's universal desire to correct the wrong doing of previous generations. And this is the Merton who understood so much about the anxiety of a post-war, Cold War world that seems so similar to the world of my students.

In his introduction to *The Seven Storey Mountain*, Robert Giroux explains that the book "appeared at a time of great disillusion…and the public was depressed and disillusioned, looking for reassurance."[19] In the wake of the Great Depression, the Second World War, the arrival of the atomic bomb, and the dawn of the Cold War, Americans were wracked with anxiety and uncertainty. Surely, the book delivers a profound message of hope for troubled times. My students today exhibit this same sense of fear and frustration. They worry about terrorism, war, and impending wars. They fret over the economy, yet often seem lost in an avaricious consumer society. In a campus culture where the possibility of being shot is a very real threat, it is no exaggeration to say that some of them are convinced they may not live to be thirty. In the wake of September 11th, when their generation was changed in an instant, many of them feel there is little purpose in old values and traditions. Yet they do not seem to believe that the answer lies in hedonism; instead, I think they are looking for something lasting. Like Merton, they understand paradox, and paradoxically, they sense that perhaps the antidote to their own sense of dread lies in the oldest spiritual truths we know. Merton's work is brimming with great themes of assurance and comfort. At the same time, as Monica Furlong has written, "what also appeal[s]...[is] the note of heroism, of idealism, of reckless self-sacrifice for a cause...and many of the young were profoundly influenced by [Merton's] example."[20]

My undergraduate students are in many ways like Merton's own novices when he served as Master of Scholastics. Merton's students, he once remarked, "come in with the jitters in the first place. They come in with a false notion of the monastic life."[21] Likewise, my students worry so much about the trivialities of grade point averages and time management that they risk missing the point of reading Merton. So, like Merton, who wrote of his students "the novices here have their breviaries full of very sad holy cards, and I am secretly planning to descend on them, take away all their favorite trash, and impose on them something good,"[22] I also want to give my students something of substance. For many of my students, Merton's work is difficult. It is full of references to places unknown and in the early books, especially, includes obscure and non-translated quotations in Latin and other languages. It references a religious tradition, and a way of life, that is absolutely foreign to them. But these are attributes that in my mind further strengthen the argument that Merton should be taught in the undergraduate college curriculum. They are the attributes that, coupled with Merton's gift for language and his keen insights into the great folly and great potential of human life, open students' intellect, emotions, and imagination to a new world.

DAVID A. KING

Some approaches to teaching Merton

Google "Thomas Merton syllabus" and you will quickly find that Merton is being taught, and he is being taught well and widely. You will also discover, however, that most of the teaching is being done in seminaries, in graduate theology programs, and as a small part of broader courses on religious studies or contemporary Christianity. What I propose is different from these approaches, for I suggest that Merton can be taught not only as a religious or Christian writer, but as an important American Writer. Besides the obvious place he could take in courses on social justice or pacifism, Merton can be taught under the umbrella of many different literary contexts which I have already described. He could be included in a course on the Beats, in a course that examines the work of more mainstream writers who came of age after World War II, or in a course that reads the work of modern American and British Catholic writers. I have taught Merton in all of these contexts, but I still believe that Merton is best taught in a course that is dedicated solely to him and his primary works. The other contexts will naturally arise as the course develops. For students to really grasp the essence of Merton, they need to devote themselves almost exclusively to his work. The course that I will describe, then, treats Merton first as a writer of literary merit who deserves inclusion in the canon of American letters. It also considers Merton's life, and specifically his monastic vocation, as worthy of serious biographical and other scholarly research. If the course has a loftier purpose than simply exposing students to the primary work of the writer, it also proposes that the work has crucial lessons to teach students about how they might pursue their own vocations and live their own lives. I teach Merton under the twofold assumption that what Merton has to say is beautiful, and that it is said beautifully. My students then see that Merton was indeed a monk, but that he was also a literary artist; they learn that Merton's outward way of living was inseparable from his inner vocation as a writer whose work was always informed by prayer.

I assume that anyone who proposes to teach a course in Merton should be equipped with a few very basic tools, the same qualifications that any instructor brings to any course, and chief among them is a knowledge of and affinity for the work. This goes beyond, I think, a reading of one or two primary titles, but does not necessarily require having read everything Merton wrote. I think the teacher of Merton, like any good teacher of any subject, will do a better job of teaching if she begins with the belief that she also has something more to learn. I also believe that because of the spiritual nature of Merton's work, the teacher of Merton should have a faith tradition of his own. He does not have to be a Roman Catholic, nor does he have to be a Christian, but he should follow in some manner a religious approach to life, and he should have some basic understanding of the religious beliefs Merton held. In this way, it is also essential that he have an ecumenical outlook, for he is not only teaching the religious view of Merton, he is also empathizing with the inevitable varied religious beliefs of his students. Finally, I think the teacher who proposes a course on Merton in a public or other secular institution needs to be able to defend Merton as a writer who can be taught based on the merits of the work alone. Although the way Merton's life and vocation developed is crucial and essential to a reading of his work, one has to be able to assert the value of his writing in a context beyond religion and religious life. Merton was a fine writer before he became a monk, and though he became a greater writer while he was a monk, the work also endures as the unique personal vision of a man who lived in other contexts, too. The teacher has to present Merton as a monk, but she has to present him in other ways as well so that the work is read and understood as literature. If the teacher cannot present Merton's work as capable of transcending a religious or monastic context, then Merton and his writings are forever susceptible to the constraints the academy has imposed for decades. If the academy can make way for the *regional* writer, the *comic* writer, the *queer* writer, it can certainly make a place for the religious writer, but the writer has to be proven first as a *good* writer.

My Thomas Merton course begins with the book that established Merton as such a writer. In the minds of many Merton scholars, *The Seven Storey Mountain* has become an elementary text, merely the first published work of an emerging talent who would become much more open and aware as he matured in his monastic and artistic vocation. But there is really no better place to begin than here when teaching Merton to a young audience essentially ignorant of his life and work. Although Merton often apologized for the book's piety, and admitted to being embarrassed by passages that smack of Catholic exclusivity, the book remains a classic example of spiritual autobiography and a fascinating portrait of one young man's pilgrimage out of doubt and despair. In the 50th Anniversary edition of the book, William H. Shannon takes pains to remind readers that "at the time Merton wrote his book, Roman Catholic theology had become a set of prepackaged responses to any and all questions. Polemical and apologetic in tone, its aim was to prove that Catholics were right and all others wrong."[23] Shannon also reminds readers that "the Roman Catholic Church you encounter in this book is almost light years removed from the church that we recognize as the Roman Catholic Church today," and assures that "readers today will be better able to put this narrowness in historical perspective and thus be less bothered by it."[24] Although I occasionally do have students who, as one put it, are "put off" by Merton's tone, for the most part students are fascinated not only by the book's depiction of the Church and monastic life but also by Merton's zeal for his ongoing conversion. As one of my students exclaimed, "I can't believe I read this book in college!" By the time they have finished *The Seven Storey Mountain*, a text to which I usually devote the first three weeks of the semester, the students become like so many other readers who first meet Merton here: they are ready for more.

Once the students have finished this first book, I set them free to read independently and casually selections of their choosing from Thomas P. McDonnell's revised *A Thomas Merton Reader*. Although this book is organized in a rather peculiar manner, it remains the best single text to acquaint new readers with Merton's astonishing range of work. While they are reading, and formulating questions, I use class time to screen several films, beginning with Paul Wilkes and Audrey L. Glynn's *Merton: A Film Biography*. Morgan Atkinson's recent documentary *Soul Searching: The Journey of Thomas Merton* also works well as an introduction and overview and further encourages the students to pursue their own private reading. Next, I show Robert G. Maier's documentary *Trappist*, which intersperses a historical overview of monasticism alongside fascinating glimpses of daily life at Mepkin Abbey in South Carolina. Following the screening of these three short films, which take up about a week of class time, the students and I return to a discussion of what they have been reading. By this point in the course, there are always plenty of questions! As the course progresses, I do make room for two more films. When we discuss the poetry, I always have the students read together and aloud Merton's long prose poem, "Original Child Bomb."

I follow this reading with a screening of Holly Becker and Carey Schonegevel's excellent film adaptation of the poem. This is one of the most stunning films I have ever shown a college audience. Each time I screen it, students are rendered speechless.[25] Finally, I always make time for Philip Groning's brilliant *Into Great Silence*, which is an essentially silent portrayal of a French Carthusian monastery.

As I have said, we are fortunate on my campus to be only about an hour's drive from the Monastery of the Holy Spirit in Conyers, Georgia, and I simply cannot imagine teaching Merton without utilizing this splendid resource. The students and I make a day trip together to the monastery; I arrange in advance an audience with a monk, followed by lunch with him in the Guest House. I encourage students to bring a friend or family member with them, and a few do. (I know the monks are delighted by how much money they all spend in the gift shop!) I am pleased at how most of my students buy copies of Merton's books. Although I understand many faculties will not have access to this type of resource, I do encourage instructors to think of other ways they can bring to the course a guest from a religious community. This might be a priest, who offers a brief lecture on the Church and the sacraments; it might be a religious from a non-cloistered community, such as the Franciscan Friars who are sometimes gathered near college campuses; it could even be a visit to the campus Catholic Center or Newman House, or for that matter a visit to a local mass or perhaps a talk from a member of another contemplative tradition. The point is to allow students to experience personally and first hand at least a glimpse of Merton's kind of life. At the same time, many of the students' prejudices or stereotypes about religious and contemplative life will be swept away.

Although I do find a period of independent reflective reading to be valuable, I also prescribe some texts that all of us read together. I almost always use both *Conjectures of a Guilty Bystander* and *New Seeds of Contemplation*; each book represents Merton's growing awareness of the world outside the monastery as well as his developing view of contemplation and action, and the voice in each is a refreshing departure from that of *The Seven Storey Mountain*. These books are a revelation, particularly for students who have developed a foundation and understanding of who Merton was and what he did. I shall never forget the student who literally burst into tears of joy, in the classroom, after reading for the first time the marvelous "Fourth and Walnut" passage from *Conjectures*. Because students are so fascinated now by Eastern religion, and because I want to emphasize the ecumenical expansion of Merton's vocation and world view, I also usually have the students read the posthumous *Asian Journal*. These three books, alongside *The Seven Storey Mountain* and the McDonnell *Reader*, are essentially all the students have time to fully absorb in a sixteen-week semester. I do provide them with a bibliographic overview of the letters, journal books, and other posthumous writing and scholarship, and I make them aware of the excellent formative studies by Michael Mott, Monica Furlong, and Victor A. Kramer. By the time we finish the semester, most of the students are ready to begin an independent study of a writer whose primary work has enthralled them. In many instances, Merton's work has also changed their lives.

There are two primary principles that I think have to inform the delivery of a course in Merton. For one, faculties have to be willing to be quiet. A Merton course offered by a droning, talking head behind a lectern will have little effect upon students. Instead of lecturing, the instructor needs to facilitate discussion, provoke questions from students, and talk *with* them rather than *at* them. The most difficult aspect of this approach is encouraging an affinity for silence. Early in the semester, I demonstrate for my students how difficult it is to be still. All of us in the academy, faculty as well as students, have become so engrained in the traditional approach to teaching and learning that for most of us a moment of silence is at the least awkward and is often perceived as a failure on the part of the teacher. I tell my students that in the absence of sound, there is often a great presence. I illustrate this sometimes by showing the wonderful moment from Godard's film *A Band of Outsiders* when the film abruptly goes silent for about forty seconds and the audience is literally obliged to listen to the absence of sound. At other times, the students and I simply sit quietly, sometimes for a moment, sometimes for several minutes. And I often offer silent periods in class for the students to write reflective responses or journal entries about the work we have been discussing. After a few weeks, the students and I are comfortable being still, and we also have built a sense of community based on mutual trust.

The second principle is to begin the course with the understanding that it is impossible in one semester to cover everything Merton accomplished. The amount of work Merton produced is astonishing, and the teacher who attempts to "get it all in" misses the rewards of treating in depth a small offering of material rather than a smattering of everything. And this is how I think the most successful teacher of Merton will perceive her role: *she is offering a gift.* My student who wept with joy at Merton's beautiful realization that he was, above all, "a member of the human race"[26] had obviously experienced a moment that left her changed. The shy student in the corner, who almost never spoke, but one day brightened the room with his assertion that like Merton he too had glimpsed "the cosmic dance,"[27] opened all of his fellow students' eyes to the truth that analysis, understanding, and theoretical posturing sometimes must give way to a simple acceptance of the sheer mystery of life. And all of my students who stand in the nave of the austere monastic church at Conyers and cease, for just a moment, the clamor of the outside world have experienced what Merton meant by describing a presence and "companionship that is tremendous...in whom are all the beauty and substance and actuality of everything in the world that is real."[28]

Could anything else offered in the contemporary American university be finer? Or more dangerous? The cynics may raise their eyebrows; the theorists and pundits may cringe, but the students and you, their teacher, will know that even in the often dreary and mundane halls of modern academia, there endures the quiet presence of grace. Teaching Thomas Merton in a public, secular setting has renewed not only my faith in the value of humane letters, it has strengthened my own sense of teaching as a vocation and quieted the onset of the skepticism so many academics succumb to at mid career. It has deepened the sense of belonging my students must have if they really seek a true education. When Merton wrote that the "the whole illusion of a separate holy existence is a dream"[29] he effectively issued an invitation for inclusion and awareness that has too long been ignored in traditional academe. Merton knew that all of us belong to one another, and though he wrote of his own work that "you should be able to share things with others without bothering too much about how they like it, either, or how they accept it. Assume they will accept it, if they need it,"[30] the contemporary university risks losing a great treasure in missing Thomas Merton.

Notes

1. Merton, Thomas, *The Seven Storey Mountain*, 50th Anniversary Edition (New York: Harcourt Brace, 1998), pp. 165-66.
2. Ibid, p. 196.
3. Ibid, p. 197.
4. This quote and all student comments that follow are taken from student essays. They have been edited only for spelling.
5. Merton, Thomas, *The Waters of Siloe*, Image Books Edition (Garden City, NJ: Image, 1962), p. 17.
6. Bochen, Christine M., "From Monastery to University: Teaching Thomas Merton to Undergraduates," *America* 159, no. 11 (1988): p. 280.
7. For more on my experience teaching *The Seven Storey Mountain*, and for more insights on approaches to teaching Merton, see also my essay in *The Merton Annual* volume 16: "Merton's New Novices: *The Seven Storey Mountain* and Monasticism in a Freshman Seminar." Continuum, 2003, pp. 73-84.
8. These examples are taken from *The Norton Anthology of American Literature* volumes I and II, the fifth edition, 1998.
9. For more on this context, see my review essay in the symposium on *Run to the Mountain* in *The Merton Annual*, Volume 9 (Collegeville, MN: The Liturgical Press, 1999), pp. 303-13.
10. O'Connor, Flannery, *Wise Blood* (New York: Farrar, Straus, Giroux, 1952), p. 218.
11. Ibid, p. 224.
12. Merton, Thomas, *The Seven Storey Mountain*, p. 453.
13. Ibid, p. 409.
14. Merton, Thomas, *The Waters of Siloe*, pp. 20-21.
15. McDonnell, Thomas P., ed. *A Thomas Merton Reader* (New York: Image, 1989), p. 16.
16. Ibid, p. 180.
17. Ibid, p. 181.
18. Ibid, p. 180.
19. Giroux, Robert, "Introduction" in Merton, *The Seven Storey Mountain*, p. xvi.
20. Furlong, Monica, *Merton: A Biography* (San Francisco: Harper and Row, 1980), p. 156.
21. Hart, Brother Patrick, OCSO, ed. *The School of Charity: The Letters of Thomas Merton on Religious Renewal and Spiritual Direction* (New York: Farrar, Straus, Giroux, 1990), p. 58.
22. Ibid, p. 109.
23. Shannon, William H., "A Note to the Reader" in Merton, *The Seven Storey Mountain*, p. xx.
24. Ibid, pp. xx-xxi.
25. For more on my reaction to *Original Child Bomb*, see my review of the film in *The Merton Annual*, Volume 19. Continuum, 2006, pp. 407-10.
26. Merton, Thomas, *Conjectures of a Guilty Bystander* (New York: Image, 1968), pp. 156-7.
27. Merton, Thomas, *New Seeds of Contemplation*, Shambhala Library Edition (Boston: Shambhala, 2003), p. 302.
28. Merton, Thomas, *The Waters of Siloe*, p. 21.
29. Merton, Thomas, *Conjectures of a Guilty Bystander*, p. 157.
30. McDonnell, Thomas P., *A Thomas Merton Reader*, p. 17.

A BIBLIOGRAPHICAL NOTE
Merton's Complete Journal as Emblem of the Spiritual Journey

Victor A. Kramer and Glenn Crider

Merton's journals, which are published in fifteen different volumes, all of which are in print, are a very important resource about him for today's readers and spiritual seekers. While no explicit examination of Merton's three decades-long project of intense journal writing is provided within either of these current *CrossCurrents* issues, these pages are fundamental to understanding him. This voluminous journal as an emblem of the twentieth century seeker's pilgrimage is crucial.

Merton was an artist and an enthusiastic convert who became a compassionate contemplative standing at the Abyss of God's Love. His journal is an exceedingly important part of that history. The journals from 1939 to 1968, unlike Thoreau's sometimes tedious recounting of a familiar path day-by-day, or the detailed daily reports of Samuel Pepys's observations, provide us not with a "record of a soul" such as John XXIII's notes. Rather, Merton's journal records his continuing struggle with the vocation he embraced and redefined. Such is the job of all of us who struggle within a post-Christian culture to balance a call from God and our call to society.

Merton's vocation was to seek a closer union with God, while in the process he affirmed the mystery of living through the surprising twentieth century. To compare this Thomas Merton as chronicler, to the figure of the "failure" portrayed in Henry Adams's *The Education of Henry Adams* might well be appropriate. Adams noted that he was born, in 1838, in the nineteenth century, yet educated in the eighteenth century while he was forced to live in the twentieth. Merton, with the temperament of Gerard Manley Hopkins and the strength of John Henry Newman, as well as the inquisitiveness of a Werner Heisenberg was born into the twentieth century, yet to a large degree he was educated in the nineteenth. His vast letter writing and sustained journal prove this. He found the leisure to examine his changing world. His prophetic contemplative stance became one of a person who is living for the twenty-first century. Thus, he remains important on many different levels: as writer, believer, poet, priest, teacher, ecumenist, and cultural critic.

In his densely packed autograph journals, a spiritual record of his journey toward a God of mercy is lovingly revealed. These 3,500 (seven volumes) record this aspiring writer/lover's engagement with the wonder of life and living as well as his simultaneous engagement year-by-year as he clarified what it meant for him to be a contemplative within this secular culture.[1] To read these journals is to see the writer being a truly committed Christian, open not just to Church and Christ, but always becoming ever more open to all persons and all cultures over which the Holy Spirit broods. This is quite apparent in each of the four volumes that Merton prepared for the press.[2]

Together Merton's fifteen different journal volumes constitute an elaborate mosaic which suggests his continuing sustained spiritual journey. These many entries are clearly, as well, a collection of resources for future readers and scholars.

Notes

1. Merton's seven volumes of autograph journals were published posthumously: *Run to the Mountain, 1939–1941*; *Entering the Silence, 1942–1952*; *Seeking Solitude, 1953–1959*; *Turning Toward the World, 1960–1963*; *Dancing in the Water of Life, 1964–1965*; *Learning to Love, 1966–1967*; and *The Other Side of the Mountain, 1968*. These journals constitute approximately thirty-five hundred pages in print. Selections were edited by Patrick Hart and Jonathan Montaldo as *The Intimate Merton*. All these books are published by HarperSanFrancisco.

2. Merton edited and revised selections of his journal as *Secular Journal*; *The Sign of Jonas*; *A Vow of Conversation*; and *Conjectures of a Guilty Bystander*. Three other selections from his journals of 1968 were also edited posthumously. These are (1) *The Alaskan Journal*; (2) *Woods, Shore, & Desert*; (3) *The Asian Journal*.

BOOKS

William Apel
Signs of Peace: The Interfaith Letters of Thomas Merton.
Foreword by
Paul M. Pearson (Maryknoll, NY: Orbis, 2006)
pp. xxi + 202. ISBN 13: 978-1-57075-681-8 (paperback). $19.00.

In an icon over my desk, Thomas Merton, portrayed wearing the Cistercian cowl, sits in a Zen position. With great serenity, Merton unites two spiritual trajectories. With his raised right hand he seems to recall Jesus saying in a number of contexts, "do not be afraid" or "peace be with you."[1] With his left hand pointed down, Merton seems to recall the Buddha saying, "Be mindful." On the back of the icon, an inscription observes that Merton pointed a way forward in this time of profound cultural change, and danger.

As William Apel states in his preface, Thomas Merton corresponded with people around the world, especially during the last years of his life, a period when four books on Asian religions appeared: *Gandhi on Non-Violence* (1965), *The Way of Chuang Tzu* (1965), *Mystics and Zen Masters* (1967), *Zen and the Birds of Appetite* (1968) plus the *Asian Journal* (1973). Merton's approach to dialogue was experiential rather than dogmatic, as suggested in a passage in *Conjectures of a Guilty Bystander*:

> If I can unite *in myself* the thought and the devotion of Eastern and Western Christendom, the Greek and the Latin Fathers, the Russians with the Spanish mystics, I can prepare in myself the reunion of divided Christians. From that secret and unspoken unity in myself can eventually come a visible and manifest unity of all Christians...We must contain all divided worlds in ourselves and transcend them in Christ.[2]

Merton saw his study of the world's religions and his engagement with a great variety of people as a contribution in the direction of world peace and unity. He received correspondents at the Abbey of Gethsemani; he visited some elsewhere, whether in New York City—Daisetz T. Suzuki (1964)—or in Asia (1968). Most, however, he never met. As a spiritual discipline he encouraged his interfaith friends to embrace others, that they too might unite in themselves and experience in their own lives all that is best and most true in the numerous spiritual traditions, "a kind of arduous and unthanked pioneering."[3]

After an introductory chapter on Merton's life of letters, Apel organizes his book around a cluster correspondents chosen for the depth and variety of their religious experiences: Abdul Aziz (Muslim), Amiya Chakravarty (Hindu), John Wu (Chinese), Abraham Heschel (Jew), D. T. Suzuki (Buddhist), Glenn Hinson (Protestant Christian), Thich Nhat Hahn (Buddhist), June Yungblut (Religious Society of Friends), and Dona Luisa Coomaraswamy (Roman Catholic with Jewish origins). Each chapter introduces the friend, a theme specific to each individual and the text of a significant letter by Merton to that individual. Notes and bibliography guide readers to such literature as Rob Baker and Gray Henry, eds., *Merton and Sufism* (1999), Beatrice Bruteau, ed., *Merton and Judaism* (2003), or Robert H. King, *Thomas Merton and Thich Nhat Hanh* (2003).

For twenty-first century persons of faith, Apel has lifted up the most urgent contribution, perhaps, of Merton, who wrote,

> If I had no choice about the age in which I was to live, I nevertheless have a choice about the attitude I take and about the way and the extent of my participation in its living ongoing events. To choose the world is not then merely a pious admission that the world is acceptable because it comes from the hand of God. It is first of all an acceptance of a task and a vocation in the world, in history and in time. In my time, which is the present. To choose the world is to choose to do the work I am capable of doing, in collaboration with my brother [and sister], to make the world better, more free, more just, more livable, more human. And it has now become transparently obvious that mere automatic "rejection of the world" and "contempt for the world" is in fact not a choice but the evasion of choice. [Those] who pretend [they] can turn [their] back on Auschwitz or Viet Nam [or Iraq, Darfur...] and act as if they were not there [are] simply bluffing.[4]

Providing an excellent introduction to interfaith pioneers, Apel has written a satisfying book. Each chapter stands on its own and can be read separately, for example, by a study group. My main source of disappointment is the absence of letters by Merton's correspondents, a strength of volumes edited by Mary Tardiff, *At Home in the World: The Letters of Thomas Merton and Rosemary Radford Ruether* (1995), Robert Faggen, *Striving towards Being: the Letters of Thomas Merton and Czeslaw Milosz* (1997); and Patrick Hart, *Survival or Prophecy? The Letters of Thomas Merton and Jean Leclercq* (2002).

–Paul R. Dekar

Notes

1. Mark 5: 36 (healing of Jairus' daughter) or John 20:19 (Jesus to disciples after the resurrection); on Merton and fear as a source of war, "The Root of War is Fear," originally published in *The Catholic Worker*, October 1961. A version appeared as Chapter 16 of *New Seeds of Contemplation* (New York: New Directions, 1962).
2. Merton, Thomas, *Conjectures of a Guilty Bystander* (Garden City, NY: Doubleday, 1966), p. 12.
3. Shannon, William H., ed., *The Hidden Ground of Love: The Letters of Thomas Merton on Religious Experience and Social Concerns* (New York: Farrar, Straus, Giroux, 1985), p. 126; letter to Dona Luisa Coomeraswamy, January 13, 1961.
4. Merton, Thomas, *Contemplation in a World of Action* (New York: Doubleday, 1971), p. 149.

Thomas Merton
Cold War Letters.
Edited by
**Christine M. Bochen and
William H. Shannon.
Foreword by James W. Douglass**
(Maryknoll, NY: Orbis, 2006),
pp. xxxiv + 206. ISBN 13: 978-1-57075-662-7 (paperback). $16.00.

The appearance of this volume more than forty years after Merton wrote the letters requires some explanation. During the year October 1961 to October 1962, Merton wrote a number of articles and a book manuscript in which he spoke out against war and for peace. Merton's awakening to a prophetic vocation of prayer and writing for the abolition of war and creation of cultures of peace arose from his vocation as monk and writer. Grounded in a deep appreciation of God's presence within him and all persons, Merton believed that his faith could not serve "merely as a happiness pill. It has to be the Cross and the Resurrection of Christ" (#3, p. 13).

By April 1962, Merton's superiors forbade him to publish on the subject of war. In obedience, he took up other writing projects; as a result, the book did not appear in his lifetime.[1] However, Merton recognized that the threat humanity faced required that he continue to work for the abolition of war as a monk and writer. He prayed. He published a few articles under pseudonyms or in obscure publications. He wrote letters to his wide circle of friends and contacts and then selected, had mimeographed and disseminated forty-nine Cold War Letters in April 1962, increased to 111 in January 1963, marked, "strictly confidential. Not for publication." This allowed Merton both to comply with the ban, and to be heard in relation to war and peace.[2]

What did Merton want to say to his correspondents? In her introduction, Christine Bochen summarizes his message: "Simply put war is the most critical issue of our day and we need, with all the resources available to us, to work to abolish war and build peace" (p. xxvi). In Merton's words, "The issue is too serious. This is purely and simply the crucifixion over again. Those who think there can be a just cause for measures that gravely risk leading to the destruction of the entire human race are in the most dangerous illusion, and if they are Christian they are purely and simply arming themselves with hammer and nails to crucify and deny Christ" (#1, p. 10).

Living physically apart from the world, Merton urged those "in the world" to understand the forces producing a "Cold War mentality," notably propaganda and technology. He urged correspondents not succumb to a "progressive deadening of conscience" (#19, p. 48) but rather to live more simply (#12, p. 33) and to seek an inner transformation (#25, p. 59).

Believing that there is that of God in every person, Merton supported peaceful exchanges with the so-called enemy and even sought some way to participate in a "peace hostage exchange" (#111, p. 193). He encouraged "non-violent and civil-disobedience movements" but warned that such movements must be disciplined rather than a form of rebellious "beatnik nonconformism" (#52, p. 106).

A generation of peace activists inspired by Merton in the sixties widened the scope of Christian non-violence. Does Merton have anything to say today? Crucially, Merton reminds us that when atomic bombs fell on Hiroshima and Nagasaki, the problem of seeking and keeping world peace ceased to be a social concern among many; it became the dominant problem not simply for Merton (who penned some of these letters amidst the Cuban missile crisis) and his generation, but also for ours. Failure to solve it means the end of seekers and solutions. Britain, China, France, India, Israel, Pakistan, Russia, and the United States possess arsenals of nuclear weapons. North Korea, Iran, and others may join the nuclear club. There are other dangers: highly carcinogenic plutonium is a health risk; enriched uranium may become accessible to nuclear terrorists.

Readers today may draw wisdom from Merton's faith, trusting God not to make us infallible but to protect us from serious error. As Merton counseled, let us listen to God and try to avoid illusions about the nature of "this great moral and spiritual challenge" (#90, p. 161). Although these letters have previously been accessible in the five volumes of Merton's letters, under the general editorship of William H. Shannon, reading this book tells us what politicians, the media and others do not (#88, p. 155). Along with the suppressed book and anthologies of Merton's social essays,[3] it is a great benefit to have the letters in a single volume, with an appendix providing biographical information about the original recipients of the *Cold War Letters*.

Merton's message to readers still governed by those who can annihilate the enemy remains remarkably relevant. I trust that publication of this collection will inspire desperately needed witness against war and for peace.

–Paul R. Dekar

Notes

1. Merton, Thomas, *Peace in the Post-Christian Era*, ed. Patricia A. Burton (Maryknoll, NY: Orbis, 2004).

2. Thirty-five letters, most of them from *Cold War Letters*, were included in Part III, "Letters in a Time of Crisis," in *Seeds of Destruction* (New York: Farrar, Straus, Giroux, 1964), pp. 237–328.

3. Merton, Thomas, *Passion for Peace: The Social Essays*, ed. William H. Shannon (New York: Crossroad, 1997).

CONTRIBUTORS

Cynthia Bourgeault is an Episcopal priest, writer, and retreat leader; she is the principal guest teacher for the Contemplative Society in Victoria, British Columbia, and a core faculty member of the Spiritual Paths Graduate Institute in Aspen, Colorado, and Santa Barbara, California. She is author of several books, including *Centering Prayer and Inner Awakening*, *The Wisdom Way of Knowing*, *Chanting the Psalms*, and *Love Is Stronger than Death*.

Glenn Crider served as production manager and editorial contributor for *The Merton Annual: Studies in Culture, Spirituality, and Social Concerns*, Vols. 14–20; he has served as co-chair of the Atlanta Chapter of The International Thomas Merton Society, 2001–2003. He holds the M.Div. and Th.M. in historical theology from Emory University.

Paul R. Dekar recently retired after thirty-four years of teaching at several theological colleges, and is an independent scholar and chair of the National Council of the Fellowship of Reconciliation. Recent publications include *Creating the Beloved Community: A History of the Fellowship of Reconciliation in the United States* and *Community of the Transfiguration: Journey of a New Monastic Community*.

Emile J. Farge was educated at St. Mary's Seminary in Houston, TX from 1954 to 1961, and after ordination served in that diocese as a parish priest until 1970. After resigning he continued his education at the University of Texas and received a Ph.D. in Public Health in 1974, serving in that field until 1998, primarily in Texas and Latin America. After resigning from public health in 1998, he has engaged in business and personal study of meditation and cross-cultural spirituality.

David A. King is associate professor of English and Film Studies at Kennesaw State University in Atlanta where he has taught courses on Thomas Merton, Flannery O'Connor, and other modern Catholic writers. His work on Merton has frequently appeared in *The Merton Annual*, and he has presented numerous papers and talks on religion and spirituality in film.

Victor A. Kramer, emeritus professor of English, Georgia State University, is a founding member of The International Thomas Merton Society; founding editor of *The Merton Annual: Studies in Culture, Spirituality, and Social Concerns*, and editor of Merton's complete journal, vol. 3, *Turning Toward the World: The Pivotal Years, 1960–1963*. His book *Thomas Merton, Monk and Artist* was published by Cistercian Publications. He is a Certified Spiritual Director and teacher for Spring Hill College in Atlanta.

John Wu, Jr. is Professor Emeritus at Chinese Culture University in Taiwan. He spoke at several ITMS Meetings from 1991 to 1997 and was the keynote speaker at Colorado Springs in 1993. The 13th child of John C. H. Wu, with whom Merton had a fruitful seven-year correspondence, John Jr. and his wife, Teresa, spent a couple of days with Merton on their honeymoon camping at Gethsemani in mid-June, 1968. He is working on an English–Chinese book on Merton prayers in which he will provide commentaries.

www.ingramcontent.com/pod-product-compliance
Lightning Source LLC
Chambersburg PA
CBHW040301170426
43193CB00020B/2966